C000022013

A People on the Boil

A People on the Boil

*Reflections on June 16, 1976
and Beyond*

Harry Mashabela

GUYO BUGUNI

First published in 1987 by Skotaville Publishers
(Incorporated Association not for Gain)

This edition, published in 2006, is a co-publication between
Jacana Media (Pty) Ltd. and Guyo Buguni

Jacana Media (Pty) Ltd.
10 Orange Street
Auckland Park
Johannesburg
South Africa

Guyo Buguni
PO Box 658
Makhado
0920
South Africa

© Harry Mashabela

All rights reserved.

ISBN 1-77009-208-0
     978-1-77009-208-2

Cover design by Disturbance

Printed by CTP Books, Cape Town
Set in Bembo 11/14

Photographs courtesy of images24.co.za, *The Star* and Alf Kumalo

See a complete list of Jacana titles at www.jacana.co.za

Contents

Foreword

Harry Mashabela has given us the most vivid portrayal of the schools uprising beginning 16 June 1976. In the early stages, it was the Soweto high school children who were involved. The conflagration was to spread to other city centres in the country.

The true journalist he is, Mashabela dispassionately lays out the details about those troubled years, listens to the voices from the school children and their leaders, voices from adult politicians, from the centres of power in government and the minions of Bantu Education.

The running sore was the issue of Afrikaans which was being enforced as the medium of instruction in certain subjects: a policy cooked up by the crackpots in Pretoria controlling education. Neither the teachers nor the children would have any of it. Nor would they hear of schools re-organised according to tribal clusters. In those turbulent days Mashabela was to come face to face with the cold and bullying tactics of apartheid rule: rule by circular – messages handed down from up high to juniors, themselves little apprenticed bullies.

Mashabela's narrative indeed presents a microcosm of the larger cesspool that was South Africa's white rule whenever Africans were concerned. It comes home forcefully to us that the government would use any excuse to gun down defenseless children – to set an example for Soweto of what massacre autocratic power could unleash. Small children braved the unknown, into exile. The rulers would pursue them, even beyond exile. Secret mass burials by the police became mere routine. The parents' homes themselves were no longer safe places to which to return.

The journalist describes the rapid appearance of groupings in Soweto of students and adults in the decade of the 1970s, some older, some more recently established: Azanian People's

Organisation; Azanian Student Orginisation; Black Parents Association; Black Community Programmes; Black People's Convention; Students Representative Council; United Democratic Front; Congress of South African Students and several others. The prominent ones wanted to be known and acknowledged.

The death of Steve Biko in September of 1977 was the climax of the government's statutory brutality. Could they ever exceed this high point? The decade of murder and mayhem in 1980s confirmed for us that there was something inbred about the lust for blood as an institution.

Although he does not dwell on it, Harry Mashabela's own detention and torture, leaving him a permanent fracture in the neck, is one of bitter ironies of autocratic rule. Once the machinery has been set going by those in charge, the agents push their agendas independently, in the handling of detainees, without any scruples about answerability to seniors. By implication, this is what the reader learns from Mashabela's whole story.

Es'kia Mphahlele
2005

Preface

When Soweto exploded on Wednesday 16 June 1976, I was covering for *The Star* the local high school pupils' protest march, called specifically to demonstrate opposition to the use of Afrikaans as medium of instruction in schools, within the complex. The severity of that explosion was so stark it nagged at me for days on end. Here was a generation of children, all of them products of an education literally intended to get them to make peace with their man-made lowly station in life, rising up in their thousands against the very authority that conceived it! I was, as it were, moved to the marrow.

Although the original work focuses on the 1976 uprising and the background to it, as well as its effects, this updated reprint goes far beyond reflections on Soweto. It covers the 1980s, the period when South Africans generally and black people in particular grappled with the task of formulating a system of education that would not only be an alternative to the prevailing divisive education systems, but would also be relevant to the envisaged non-racial democratic South Africa. It needs to be said, too, that the book is not a treatise on black politics in South Africa, but rather a human story: the story of a people trapped in a wicked system and fighting to wriggle out to free themselves.

Several factors facilitated production. First, there were the Soweto community leaders who invited me even to their private meetings where they grappled with problems of the day; then the many individuals in and outside Soweto who willingly gave interviews. Without their trust and co-operation, it might have been utterly impossible to capture the climate, the mood within which this overwhelming human story occurred. And for all this, I'm grateful in no small way to each and every one of them. Also, the fact that the national press was covering events as they unfolded elsewhere enabled me to keep abreast with what went on countrywide. For this reprint, may I express special gratitude to Maano Tuwaani, director of Guyo Book Services, whose belief in and insistence on the need for the book to be reprinted always encouraged me, and library consultant and bibliographer Abdul Bemath, who gave valuable advice regarding research for material relevant to this update.

Except for the deliberate name omissions and use of pseudonyms here and there, nothing in this book is fictional. The story is as factual and accurately told as I could do it – to the best of my ability. And I take full responsibility for everything in the work.

Harry Mashabela
2006

CHAPTER I

STORM CLOUDS GATHERED

On Wednesday, 16 June 1976, the sun rose earlier – as always – in Soweto than elsewhere in the world. It rose at three-thirty when workers, roused from sleep before they were fully rested, scuttled out of their homes on the way to railway stations to catch first trains to work.

Thus most of the people lingering in the streets at daybreak were children. Only a sprinkling of adults, who didn't have to leave home before daybreak, moved about. They hurried to railway stations or restlessly waited in small groups at different points for buses and taxis. In contrast, the pupils seemed calmer, more cheerful as they went along. Soweto, snuggled within a film of smoke, looked dull despite the agitated movements in the streets. But as the morning grew older and older with virtually every minute, if not second, the air cleared. So much so that even a stranger roaming the ghetto could have seen, no matter the distance, the Urban Bantu Council chamber that dwarfed the myriad, symmetrical tiny cottages housing inhabitants, the Orlando Power Station and, perhaps, the Oppenheimer Tower as well.

Approximately five hundred pupils crowded under the shadow of Thomas Mofolo Junior Secondary School in Naledi, a suburb of the vastness called Soweto, at about seven-thirty. As they stood there, clustered like a swarm of bees, the pupils held a meeting. No teachers were in sight. Nor were they anywhere within the school premises. The passers-by did not seem to take particular notice of the gathering.

At Naledi High School, about a mile away, principal Nathan Molope, a pastor and veteran school teacher, stood hands clasped behind his back outside his office. He stared blankly into the air, giving his back to the dull early morning sun as if to warm his hands. Students lingered within the premises. Some went in and out of classrooms, some hung around in tiny groups chatting, laughing. He seemed to be deep in thought.

The bell for morning assembly rang. More students streamed out of the classrooms. They joined groups outside. They produced posters or placards from under their clothes. They unfurled them amid intermittent cries: 'Power! Away with Afrikaans' and 'Free Azania! Power!' Then they moved in a rather confused column not to the assembly quadrangle but towards the main gate. Molope did not know what was happening, he said.

'As you can see,' he added in afterthought, 'there's trouble.' He pointed out a thick-set youngster marshalling the student body, nearly seven-hundred-strong, into Nyakale Street below. 'He might tell you what's going on,' the principal said.

Tebello Motapanyane, a student leader at the school and also secretary-general of the South African Students Movement (Sasm), darted backwards and forwards, urging students to get to the streets. Brandishing placards and shouting slogans, they poured into the tarred road, blocking traffic and marching towards Naledi Hall. Tebello said that they were going to Thomas Mofolo Junior Secondary, whence they would march to Phefeni Junior Secondary, about six miles away. The air was pregnant with excitement. Younger school children, cheering, watched from roadsides. A white photographer tried to get a shot. Tebello saw him, rushed and, gesticulating, warned him not to do anything of the sort. Pictures would get them into trouble with the police. The photographer backed into his car. Tebello dashed back, joining the march.

Morris Isaacson High School in Central West Jabavu was already deserted. A crude sign 'No SBs [security branch police] allowed.

Enter at your own risk' hung at the gate. A group of teachers sat forlornly in front of the laboratory at the southern wing of the school. The headmaster was not among them. His students, eight hundred of them, had gone to Phefeni, said his deputy, Norman Malebane.

Earlier that morning events at the school had been unusual, to say the least. As the assembly bell rang at 8am students hurriedly gathered together and, led by Tsietsi Mashinini, enthusiastically broke into song: '*Masibulele ku Jesu; ngokuba wa sifela* (Let's pray Jesus; for He died for us).' They sang, without waiting for Malebane who normally conducted assembly sessions. After the hymn, they sang with equal enthusiasm 'Nkosi Sikelel' i-Afrika,' the African national anthem. Malebane, who had been approaching, stopped in his tracks. He did nothing whatsoever. Thank God, he laughed, he had been warned and thus did not want to interfere. That would have been disastrous. It would have brought a lot of trouble for him. Still singing the national anthem and waving placards, they marched out of school grounds into Mphuthi Street, leaving startled teachers behind.

Two days earlier Lekgau Mathabane, the lanky headmaster of Morris Isaacson, who was the executive committee member of the African Teachers Association of South Africa (ATASA), Cripple Care Association, Parents Vigilante Committee and chairman of the Post-primary School Principals Union, had disclosed that Soweto high school students planned a public march for Wednesday. They wanted to protest in sympathy with pupils at five higher primary and junior secondary schools who had been boycotting classes for five weeks; objecting to compulsory use of Afrikaans as medium of instruction. But the school children had, as it were, caught everybody with their pants down. The public seemed to have missed the little news reports about the proposed protest march, or they considered them unimportant. But whatever the general attitude of South Africa was, the Soweto school children were dead serious and it turned out to be a momentous day, a day never to be forgotten.

From Thomas Mofolo the column, which had started at Naledi High but was almost doubled, marched down Mphatlalatsane Street in the southern part of the township. They still chanted freedom songs and shouted slogans amid the raucous rallying cry: 'Power! Power!' The ranks of the march were swelling all the time as younger children, who didn't even know what it was all about, joined the column.

Flanked by his lieutenants, some wielding sticks and knobkerries, Tebello led the column. Across the rivulet within the hollowed open space cutting Naledi from Tladi the column swung left. It moved northwards through the grassy veld at the bottom of Tladi, then right into Legwale Street. It turned eastwards. A little above, but below Tladi Clinic, waited three police cars. The huge column approached. The police officers slowly drove ahead. They turned left at the Zola/Legwale T-junction, but the march turned right towards Moletsane. The shouting and waving pupils taunted motorists travelling in the opposite direction. With open hands, they hit the cars and some motorists, frightened by the marching throng, turned back or fled into side streets.

At the top of Moletsane the march turned right towards Molapo where school children from Molapo Junior were collected. Cavorting in the streets through Jabavu and Mofolo South, they wormed down the road towards Nancefield. Then they swung left at the bottom of the Vocational Training Centre in Dube Village, the famed tourist attraction with its posh houses, some doubled-storeyed, on the way to Phefeni Junior just beyond the rugged ridge ahead.

Thousands of other students from other schools – Musi, Mncube, Sekano-Ntoana, Morris Isaacson, Meadowlands, Diepkloof and Orlando North – were already converging in

Vilakazi Street outside Phefeni Junior. Phefeni Junior pupils and those from nearby Orlando West High streamed out, some jumping over fences, to meet them. Woman columnist Lucy Gough Berger of *The Star* was caught up in the crowds around 'Beverly Hills'. She later wrote:

> *I couldn't get over their size. The boys bulked out of their clothes; the girls, legs like sturdy tree trunks beneath their gyms, squarely stood their ground... One look at the sullen expression of a group of hefty girls put paid to my idea of talking to them. A teacher from the school came to us.*
>
> *'Get that car out of here they're coming!' he urged. On the brow of the hill, in a great dusty whirlwind, a phalanx of high school kids chanting surged down the road in thousands. Below us, pupils from Phefeni began running to meet them. 'Hurry!' cried the teacher.*
>
> *Timothy, the driver, turned into the deserted long drive of Orlando West High School. The river of placard- and stick-waving pupils outside the school's meshed fence converged like two rivers of protest in an emotional embrace. That was the moment they saw me snapping away from behind a tree. A black youth of about fifteen years, with a two metre long saw-blade, thrust his face close to mine. Another pinioned me against the car.*
>
> *'What do you want?' they screamed.*
>
> *I mouthed something but nobody heard. All around were menacing clenched fists and shouts of Black Power!*
>
> *'Get out of this ground now,' roared a youth waving a whopping big stick, 'This is black property. Get out, get out white woman,' they chanted.*
>
> *It was the driver Timothy — cool, wise Timothy — whose words in that split second, while the mob hesitated, saved me. 'Leave her alone. She's from a newspaper, she is not from the*

Department of Bantu Education,' he pleaded.

'Alright Daddy, take your car and take her out of here!'

The youth with the saw-blade cleared the way like a cop while the pupils fell back a few centimetres and thumped on the windows of the hemmed-in car.

At the gate the escort ceased.

The huge crowd blocked the street. It stood almost half a mile down the road, awaiting thousands more from Naledi, Moletsane, Molapo and Emndeni. A policeman stood with a stengun cradled and a van full of dogs next to him. More police arrived in vans and trucks. They were armed and accompanied by dogs. They climbed out of the vehicles and moved behind five officers who walked side by side towards the singing throng.

CHAPTER 2

SOWETO SHAKEN

When WC Ackerman, director of Bantu Education in the southern Transvaal region which included Soweto, issued a directive late in 1974 compelling principals of schools and school boards, who administered schools, to use Afrikaans as medium of instruction from the beginning of the 1975 school term, he could not have realised he was stirring a hornet's nest. He could never have thought that there would be any resistance against his ruling. His predecessor, Dr Jacobus Bernadus de Vaal, had after all successfully introduced ethnic school boards in Soweto in 1972 despite opposition from the community.

Expressing the feelings of the parents, the mixed school boards that were to be replaced had then told Dr de Vaal that tribal school boards would not be in the interest of the people of Soweto. Almost to a man the school board representatives voiced their disquiet, but he implemented his policy, a policy deriving from the Bantu Education Department generally and in particular the South African government. Before that the government had, also through Dr de Vaal, imposed tribal schools, making sure that African children from the various ethnic groups were no longer educated side by side. Each group had to have its own schools and, subsequently, its own administrators.

The government's rigid divide–and–rule tactic, obviously aimed at frustrating any growth of national spirit among the African people, was now complete. Now that everything had been done, not only to separate Africans from whites but also Africans from

Africans along tribal lines, the master's language had to be rammed down the African child's throat.

Soweto was shaken. How could school children be expected to learn through three languages? Were English and mother tongue not sufficient handicaps? Now it must also be Afrikaans, no matter how badly qualified teachers were to handle other subjects in that language.

Some even murmured that Pretoria should be taken to court over the Afrikaans language issue. But others reckoned the move would be pointless, a sheer waste of money. Although the Bantu Education Act, the law governing African education, gave African parents some sort of authority to choose between English and Afrikaans for a medium of instruction, they said, the entire African education system was really still controlled by the whims of Michel C Botha, the minister of Bantu Administration and Development: a 'father' of all the African people, as it were, within the country. There was absolutely nothing that had happened in African education over the years to give them encouragement. Pretoria had shirked its responsibility of providing African schools in the midst of a crippling school shortage. African parents had to build schools for their own offspring out of their own meagre resources. The government had also turned down requests for a comprehensive teacher training institution for the ghetto community to tackle the problem of woefully inadequate teachers. Existing schools, crammed with pupils, had to make do with unqualified teachers. The teacher–pupil ratio in the classroom stood, on average, at one to seventy. Most pupils did not even have books because parents could not afford them. And no one had been able to shake government out of its utter indifference. The situation was quite hopeless, heart-rending.

The new directive required pupils to be taught mathematics, history and geography in Afrikaans: general science and practical subjects (homecraft, needlework, woodwork, metalwork, arts and craft) as well as agriculture in English, whilst mother tongue would be used in teaching religious education, music and physical education. What a burden! Indeed, could anyone still doubt the slave mentality among Africans? Previously, the choice between English and Afrikaans rested in the hands of the community. Mother tongue, especially at lower levels of education, was compulsory.

Parents and school principals as well as the tribal school boards saw the injunction as the brain-child of a political, not educational, motive; the last straw. Consequently, they stirred. They appealed to Ackerman to withdraw his ruling, but their pleas fell on deaf ears. Their arguments that teachers were not sufficiently qualified to handle other subjects in Afrikaans were rejected out of hand. He could not have dealt them a crueler blow. However, they refused to throw in the towel.

In August 1975, the school boards in Soweto combined forces with others outside the region. They formed the Federal Council of Transvaal School Boards under the chairmanship of Cornelius Marivate, a Pretoria resident and teacher of considerable standing in the community, so that they could speak in one voice in tackling, first and foremost, the language issue and the problem of teacher training facilities. Having failed to browbeat the school boards, Ackerman tried to drive a wedge between them and their employee teachers. He sent his circuit inspectors to schools in Soweto. Teachers were threatened they would not get salary increments nor would they be considered for senior posts if they did not comply with the official ruling.

The chairman of the Meadowlands Tswana school Board, Joseph Peele, and his deputy Abner Letlape were summarily dismissed in February 1976, apparently for being too stubborn. First, Letlape was demoted from the chairman and replaced with Peele, who had been deputy chairman. But when he too refused to implement the language ruling, the two men were fired. Meanwhile school boards representing other ethnic groups – Venda, Tsonga, Bapedi and Xhosa – had succumbed to pressures from the regional director. In response to the dismissal of Letlape and Peele, other members of the Meadowlands Tswana School Board resigned and parents supported them. A parents' public meeting even threatened to assault any person who co-operated with Ackerman and his inspectors by accepting offers to replace those who resigned. The parents also warned teachers not to teach their children in Afrikaans.

Perhaps still believing reason would prevail, the Batswana people asked Chief Lucas Mangope, chief minister of Bophuthatswana, their so-called homeland, for help. They wanted him to raise the language issue with Prime Minister Vorster. Mangope visited Voster and had an audience with him under the shadow of the Houses of Parliament in Cape Town, but his efforts were in vain. The irony was that Chief Mangope's homeland government had opted for English as medium of instruction in schools in the homeland, while the wishes of 'his people' in Soweto, like those other ethnic groups, were crippled by the South African government.

A crisis had developed. The Soweto community was disillusioned. Anger and bitterness was rife, especially among the youth. They had seen their parents fight a losing battle. What could they do about a burden that appeared too heavy even to their parents? Were they, like their parents, to accept defeat? No, some of them thought.

On 17 May pupils at Phefeni Junior School started a boycott of classes. They demanded to see circuit inspector M C de Beer, a man who had been a policeman before he was appointed inspector of African schools. When he told the school principal, Charles Mpulo, that he would not see the pupils, the angry children deflated tyres of the principal's car and stoned his office. Then De Beer gave them an ultimatum. He would, he said, expel them if they did not return to classes within three days. They did not. Instead, four other schools within the circuit joined the boycott. But Ackerman, with

Pretoria's blessing, still refused to withdraw his controversial ruling. In an editorial, *The Star* in May 1976 warned:

> *The men who made the ruling that some subjects in black schools be taught in English and Afrikaans are a menace to South Africa's security, to racial peace, and to the Afrikaans language. What they have done would cause an up-roar if it were done in white school…*
>
> *It is a cold-blooded, ideological regulation which could not do more to downgrade black education if it were designed for that purpose.*

Characteristically, nobody listened.

Two policeman – a white and a black – drove into Naledi High School grounds on Monday, 9 June to arrest a student, apparently for questioning. The principal warned them not to do so in the presence of other school kids. The policemen were still inside the principal's office when some children surrounded their car and set it alight.

On Sunday afternoon Dr Aaron Matlhare, a medical practitioner, held a parents' meeting inside Naledi Hall adjacent to his surgery. The quiet, bespectacled small man with pitch dark hair on an oblong head and a light long face, was something of a loner. He had never before shown any interest in public affairs. Accompanied by his wife, Nkele, a slender woman who was a trained nurse working with him in his surgery, Dr Matlhare was for the fist time showing his concern over developments in Soweto. Nkele, with heavy make-up and a rather towering hairdo, had perhaps come to bear witness. But the Soweto medical practitioner failed to attract many people to his meeting. Only about three hundred in a community of more than a million inhabitants turned up. And he was unconvincing in his agitation for the formation of a parents' association, a body that would tackle the problems gnawing at the heart of the community. He seemed not to have thought deeply about what he really wanted done. However, his well-intentioned but miserable attempt to rouse interest into the creation of a new body was adequately compensated for by his guest speaker, Winnie Mandela. Tall and decidedly beautiful in her tight African-print dress reaching down to her ankles, Sis Winnie, as she's popularly known, did not mince her words. She prefaced her talk with a freedom song:

> *Unzima lo mthwalo;*
> *unzima, ufuna amadoda*
> *ufuna sihlangane*
>
> *It's heavy this burden;*
> *It's heavy, it needs men,*
> *It needs unity.*

She enthused in her deep sonorous voice with the gathering joining in. Then she dug deep into her talk.

They were gathered there to rediscover themselves and their role as parents, she said. The government was doing everything in its power to divide the black people. It was sowing suspicion among blacks. Because of poverty and starvation, it found it easy to get informers, blacks who were willing to sell their own people. 'Amandla!' someone rent the hushed still air within the hall, if only to express his delight. But Sis Winnie would not be interrupted, even by an obvious supporter. She continued, agitatedly but seriously, as if she had not heard the Black Power rallying cry. A mother of two teenage girls whose father, Nelson Mandela, was serving a life prison term on Robben Island in the south sea off Cape Town, having tried as leader of the African National Congress (ANC) to secure a better future for his people, Sis Winnie stressed that the law restricting blacks ought to unite them. They carried passes not because they wanted to conform to someone's concept but because without them they could not work and marry and own and rent houses. They could not even register births without the passes.

An old man, apparently disenchanted with her sentiments, heckled. She stopped and, sulking, stared not at the howler but into the audience. Two men rose from their seats in the front row. They manhandled the heckler, bundled him out of the hall.

'I told you it's heavy this burden,' she chuckled.

They had spent almost four hundred years, she said, talking and doing nothing. Some seemed satisfied with merely talking. Their children had taken to the streets. They were fighting a war that was not really theirs but that of their parents. They found their parents wanting, unprepared to do anything. Did they still have a right to be called parents? She believed the kids despised them. They would spit on their graves because as parents they had failed to do their duty.

Black children, like those of other races, were entitled to parental love. And that placed great responsibility on parents. They could not continue doing nothing in the face of utter oppression. Something had to be done and she felt Soweto parents should form an association. Not an association of Batswana nor any other tribal group, but an association that would represent and serve all the people of Soweto. Such an association, she asserted, would attend to the Afrikaans issue now frustrating pupils.

The audience, applauding, gave her a standing ovation. The Soweto Parents Association (SPA) was born instantly. Dr Matlhare was nominated interim committee chairman. Winnie was included in the interim executive. The committee was entrusted with planning an inaugural meeting on Sunday, 27 June. As the meeting ended, people mobbed and kissed Sis Winnie. Her words had been nectar to people so long robbed of any charismatic leadership.

Open African political activities had ceased after Sharpville on 21 March 1960 when police mowed down sixty-nine anti-pass demonstrators in Vereeninging; when the main political movements – the ANC and the Pan Africanist Congress (PAC) – were outlawed. The future was bleak; white South Africa had completely shut the door, had spurned black people's concerted appeals since 1912 for acceptance and recognition. Robert Mangaliso Sobukwe, the academic who had abandoned a teaching post at the University of the Witwatersrand to lead the PAC, was arrested for organising the anti–pass campaign. He was subsequently imprisoned and kept for more than six years in detention, even after serving the three-year prison term. ANC leader Nelson Mandela, a trained lawyer, went underground whence he espoused, for the first time, violence as the only weapon against oppression within the country. That objective landed him and others in the Rivonia Trial of 1964. They were jailed for life. And that sentence put paid to whatever underground political activity had lingered after Sharpville.

It was in that vacuum that a new philosophy of Black Consciousness was born with the formation in 1968 of the African Student Organisation (Saso). A reawakening that sought to foster in black people a better, healthy self-image: to exorcise the age-old feeling of inferiority that ruined them. It frowned upon unity with whites in seeking to attain its goal, but embraced coloured and Indian people. Rather, it encouraged unity and expressed the desire to serve the interests of all those South Africans who were, by law or politically, socially, economically and of course educationally, discriminated against, purely on the basis of skin colour.

Black people were exhorted to realise that they were all alone in the struggle for a psychological liberation, and that whites were in fact part of the problem, not the solution. Blacks had not only to be proud of what they were, but also to be assertive and self-reliant. Black people were in a sense attempting to see themselves through their own eyes, and no longer through the eyes of the oppressor. Thus Saso broke ties with the white-dominated National Union of South African Students (Nusas) for young liberal university students. Only when psychological freedom had been attained, believed the young crusaders, could any useful dialogue and co-operation between black and white be entertained.

Some older folk within the black community itself, let alone whites who denounced the young movement as racist, ridiculed the youthful black students. What did they know about politics anyway? A bunch of immature, irresponsible, arrogant hot-heads bent on mischief, they cried, and attacked the young leadership for rejecting the popular stance which in the main accommodated liberal thinking. Liberal white thinking, in fact, merely abhorred the rigidity in the application of the apartheid system, but never really wanted the rot uprooted and eliminated completely. Ironically, the racist government saw the new movement, initially, as some sort of endorsement of the 'holiness' and validity of the separate development thesis simply because it rejected ties with white liberals.

Predictably, the movement was given no chance by its detractors. But led by its founder and president Steve Biko, a highly articulate, forthright and thoughtful young man with a profound sense of commitment, Saso grew from strength to strength countrywide. Biko did not only call upon adherents to preach the gospel, but also to foster black solidarity. Young men were sent into various communities where they did not only preach the word but demonstrated their commitment too by creating and running, albeit on a shoe-string, health centers and literacy campaigns. Theatres, stressing the importance of the black experience as part of black history, were established. In their wake and activities, the crusaders condemned the divisive concept of separate development and accused fellow blacks who co-operated with the system of unwittingly destroying the black nation.

Pretoria was stunned.

The young movement drew even harsher condemnation when it openly supported moves by anti-apartheid forces abroad which discouraged investments in the country. It believed foreign investment sustained the oppressive system, making it efficient even. Its leadership accepted the general notion that blacks would suffer most if investment were withdrawn, but stressed that the black people were suffering anyway. While they argued that the entire country would be adversely affected by full-scale economic sanctions, they said such a move could give hope to black aspirations. For the first time in history, black people would begin to suffer with some objective; an objective that out of their suffering might come some good. After all, whites were in a position to bring about change, in the sense that they had the vote, would know exactly why they were now suffering (for the first time in the history of South Africa) and thus be forced to make amends. They seemed particularly hurt by dishonest utterances in the pro-investment lobby that investments were aimed at helping blacks and asserted that companies invested in the country essentially because they knew they could make more profits than they could ever hope for in their own countries where trade unionism was powerful and labour expensive. Here, they exploited cheap black labour. After all, the black worker could be paid anything here, for he depended on the mercy of his employer and, as any thinking person was aware, there weren't many merciful employers around. Business people established businesses for profit, not charity.

Barely four years after its inception, Saso had spearheaded the formation of the Black People's Convention (BPC), a national black political movement intended to fill the gap created by the banning of the ANC and PAC. The dubious Association for Educational and Cultural Advancement of Africans (Asseca) had called a conference of existing black organisations at the Donaldson Orlando Community Centre (DOCC) in Orlando East, Soweto, in December 1971. Asseca's president Tom Moerane told the conference of the need for the formation of an umbrella body which would represent all cultural and educational organisations within the black community throughout the country.

But Harry Nengwekhulu, Saso's permanent organiser, was not amused. A Turfloop University graduate, Nengwekhulu swung the conference. He told the gathering that blacks were sick and tired of the multitudes of so-called cultural bodies which had mushroomed within the country but did nothing for the people. They wanted a movement which would accommodate their broad political aspirations. Moerane, the conference chairman and convenor, was incensed and tried unsuccessfully to rule Nengwekhulu out of order. Nengwekhulu, who had apparently canvassed for his idea, forced the issue to a vote. He won the day and the chairman was left in the cold.

Not only was Saso instrumental in the creation of BPC, it also shaped the movement's manifesto. The two organisations were in fact indistinguishable in policy and outlook. They both upheld the Black Consciousness thesis, but divided their spheres of operation.

While Saso was home for black university students, BPC was, on the other hand, a movement for adults. Youngsters who dropped out of school were encouraged to join BPC while those who entered university were expected to become Saso members.

Whatever image Saso had among black people was boosted in April 1972 when Professor John Boshoff, rector of Turfloop University for the North-Sotho, South-Sotho, Tswana, Venda and Tsonga ethnic groups, expelled student leader Abram Onkgopotse Tiro. A Saso activist, Tiro had scathingly attacked Bantu Education and called for meaningful reforms at the university during a graduation ceremony. A history graduate of the university (he was studying for a teacher's diploma at the time), Tiro had been asked by students to speak at the ceremony on their behalf.

He told the black and white guests attending the ceremony that black people wanted a system of education that would be common to all South Africans irrespective of colour. Often he wondered, he said, just how black lecturers at the university contributed to its administration. All the committees were predominantly white, if not completely white. Here and there one found two or three Africans who, in the opinion of students, were white black men. Students had, for instance, a dean without duties. They felt that if it were in any way necessary to have a student's dean, they should elect their dean, for they knew people who could serve them.

The university's advisory council was said to be representing parents, he continued. How could it represent them if they had not elected it? By necessity council members would represent the interests of those who appointed them. The council consisted of tribal chiefs who had never been to university. How could they know the needs of students when they had never been subjected to the same conditions? Those members who had been to university had never studied under Bantu Education. What authentic opinion could they express when they didn't know how painful it was to study under a repugnant system of education, he asked.

Tiro also wondered if the council knew that a black man had been kicked out of the university bookshop. Apparently, he said, the bookshop had been reserved for whites. However, according to policy, Van Schaick – a white company – had no right to run a bookshop on the campus. A white member of the university had also been given a contract to supply meat to the university – a black university. Those who supported the policy might say there were no black people to supply it. Tiro's answer to them was: why were the blacks not able to supply the university? Was it not convenient that there were no black people to supply these commodities?

White students, Tiro disclosed, were given vacation jobs at the university when there were black students who could not get their results due to outstanding fees. Why did the administration not give those jobs to those students? The white students had eleven universities where they could get vacation jobs. Did the administration expect him to get a vacation job at Pretoria University?

Questioning whether blacks would ever be given a fair deal in South Africa, he said that even at that very graduation ceremony his father and other parents, who had travelled from their homes to see their children graduate, were seated at the back of the hall while front seats were allocated to whites – people who could not possibly cheer the graduates. The system, he stressed, was failing because even those who recommended it strongly as the only solution to racial problems in South Africa, failed to adhere to the letter and spirit of that policy. According to policy, students expected Dr Eiselen (one of the key policy-makers who sired Bantu Education) to decline chancellorship of the university in favour of a black man.

Tiro exhorted students to accept the challenge of a liberation struggle. Their so-called leaders (homeland leaders) had become the bolts of the same machine that was crushing the black nation. The graduates had to change them. Times were changing and they should change with them. Of what use would their education be if they could not help their country in her hour of need? If their education was not linked to the entire continent of Africa, it was meaningless, he said.

Overnight, Tiro became a hero to the black people of South Africa, but a villain to the university administration. Boshoff could no longer countenance him on the campus.

Tiro was expelled. In response, students rioted and the university was closed, with the entire student body suspended. Then black campuses elsewhere in the country stirred, rallying behind Tiro and his suspended colleagues. They boycotted lectures and their universities were also closed.

The young student movement had now caught the eye of the nation. Tiro, an uncompromising young man, had become a father figure. As Turfloop University eventually re-opened without him, the entire Students Representative Council (SRC) was refused readmission and Saso activities were banned on the campus, he went to work full-time promoting Black Consciousness in the black community. Aware that the movement had become very much alive and a serious talking point in the community, the Saso executive went for the kill. Cultural bodies (among them the Soweto Black Ensemble and Mihloti) were established throughout the country's major industrial areas, specifically to enunciate feelings, emotions and hopes of ghetto life through drama; Mdali confederation of theatre and publication groups was launched to promote theatre, music, art and literature. Booklets, such as *Black Viewpoint* and *Creative and Development* were published, in addition to the regular Saso Newsletter.

To co-ordinate all youth activities in the Witwatersrand area, the Transvaal Youth Organisation was also created. And Sasm, which had been operating among high school pupils in Soweto, was encouraged by Saso activists to include other black racial groups in its ranks, to preach Black Consciousness and to concern itself with injustice within the society. It became an affiliate of the Transvaal Youth Organisation. Saso provided leadership training to high school students. Attempts to organise black workers were also mooted.

A number of students connected with Saso had, of course, graduated from university and gone into teaching in black schools. Would they stop advocating Black Consciousness now that they were teachers? Not on your life. Tiro came to teach at Morris Isaacson High in Soweto while Aubrey Mokoena, SRC president when they were expelled from Turfloop University after the Tiro affair, joined the Orlando North Secondary School teaching staff. Biko was a full-time field worker for the Black Community Programmes which organised and ran literacy campaigns and health centres at various points countrywide. Black Consciousness was entrenching itself deeply in the black community.

In a veiled attempt to punish Tiro and others who had been expelled from Turfloop, education authorities ordered school boards never to hire him and the other 'ring leaders'. The boards were warned they would not be given grants nor be allowed to use school funds to pay them. Reverend David Nkwe, an Anglican Church pastor who, until his demotion at the end of 1975, was chairman of the school board controlling Morris Isaacson, refused to heed the warning. Tiro, he contended, was employed by black parents to teach black children and he was qualified to do the job. He would pay him out of funds because the funds were raised by parents. He believed parents had the right to use the funds the way they felt necessary. He would relent only if officials told parents they didn't even have the right to use their own money to retain Tiro and would, he said, gladly arrange a meeting between officials and parents. Officials baulked. And Tiro went on teaching. But as fate would have it, the school ran out of funds and experienced difficulties in paying him; also, said school princilpal Mathabathe, Tiro himself wanted to go after some of his colleagues in the movement were banned in 1973. He said he feared he might be detained and so he left.

The year 1973 was barely four months old when Saso and BPC were virtually crippled. The government banned the following leaders for five years: Saso president Jerry Modisane, Saso secretary-general Barney Pityana, Saso permanent organiser Harry Nengwekhulu, BPC publicity officer Saths Cooper, Drake Koka, a BPC founder executive member who was involved in organising trade unions among blacks, Steve Biko and Bokwe Mafuna, both of them Black Community Programmes (BCP) field workers, in March 1973. The ban revealed once again that a people cannot really rule others unless they fully recognise and respect their humanity. It was indeed a sad moment for the Black Consciousness movement, for black South Africa. The movement's seasoned, mellow and thoughtful leadership was destroyed. For the next five years, the leaders could neither attend meetings, nor speak to the community through the media. They were silenced, totally silenced. Tiro became Saso permanent organiser, but when Nengwekhulu and Koka as well as other fellow activists fled to Botswana after the banning orders, he joined them. He died in exile on 1 February 1974 when a parcel bomb exploded in his face at St. Joseph Secondary School outside Gaborone, Botswana, where he was teaching. But Saso and BPC continued their work despite the banning and the fact that some leaders had fled from the country.

When the Afrikaans language problem hit Soweto at the beginning of 1975, representatives of the two bodies attended parents' meetings. They kept students adequately informed about developments. For a whole year parents and school boards appealed in vain to have the Afrikaans ruling rescinded. After the start of the 1976 school year, the Bantu Education regional office went out of its way to see that policy was carried out by all schools. Teachers at some schools began teaching stipulated subjects in Afrikaans as ordered by the regional director. Then students at Phefeni Junior Secondary School decided to boycott classes on 17 May. By the beginning of the next month four other schools had joined the boycott.

The Afrikaans language issue aside, African education had for decades been circumscribed. Since its inception in 1955, African education had been badly financed. It was pegged at R13–million a year. Teachers were badly paid, making the profession itself woefully unattractive. There were few libraries and laboratories, if any at all, and equipment was terribly poor. Classes were so congested that a double session system was introduced and unqualified teachers were used in an attempt to cope with the heavy pupil–teacher ratio. No free stationery and textbooks were available in spite of the agonising poverty facing the African parents. Not only was the quality of education miserably poor, but black experience also showed that good education for a black man was in many ways a liability. Often, blacks found they were 'too educated' to get employment even in industry. And even where jobs were available, rewards were minimal. In fact, black talents were not supposed to be developed to the full, nor skills used adequately. Racial discrimination held sway all round.

But education authorities still remained adamant and would not yield to the children's demand. After all they had beaten their parents to it. BPC suggested to the leadership of Sasm, the high school student movement, to show solidarity with those higher primary and junior secondary schools who boycotted classes. The suggestion was accepted and the decision to hold a protest march involving all high school children in their individual capacities as students, not as members of Sasm, was taken. That way, it was felt, the march would involve even those students who were not Sasm members. The plan for the march then began with Tsietsi Mashinini at the helm. Student meetings were held at various high schools throughout Soweto. There was support for the proposed protest march virtually everywhere.

Wednesday, 16 June was chosen as D–day.

CHAPTER 3

PEACEFUL PROTEST SOURED

The animated massive crowd crammed Vilakazi Street opposite both Phefeni Junior Secondary and Orlando West High alongside sedate 'Beverly Hills'. Standing almost half a mile deep down the road, the huge crowd blocked the entire street. Impish, buoyant, they sang and waved placards.

Five white police officers in blue uniforms stood side by side in the middle of the road about fifteen paces away and faced the sea of black faces below. Behind them more and more uniformed police, most of them black, and riot squad men, armed with rifles and accompanied by dogs, alighted from police trucks. They strode down the tarred road towards the officers and the amassed pupils. They joked among themselves as they moved on. (How else could they have felt; nothing of the sort had ever happened before.) Several women, some with babies strapped to their backs, watched in groups from the roadside. Eeriness hung in the air. 'Are you going to kill our children?' a woman in a group asked an African police sergeant as he strode past.

'No, there'll be no shooting,' said the officer calmly. 'The children are not fighting anybody; they're only demonstrating…' He was still talking when the white officer on the extreme right quickly stepped to the side, stooped down and picked what seemed to be a stone. Then he hurled the object into the crowd. Instantly, the kids in front of the column scattered to the sides. They picked up stones, then they hurriedly surged back into the street. 'P-o-w-e-r! Power!' they screamed, hesitantly advancing towards the police.

'Bang', a shot rang out; then another and yet another in rapid succession.

The throng broke up with pupils fleeing in all directions: to the rugged ridge behind the two schools, into alleyways, side streets and into homes. Some collapsed in their tracks as they fled, some ran on. Some, apparently petrified, remained in the middle of the street. The police paid no attention to them. Or so it seemed. They stared at those running away. A police dog charged at the diminishing group in the street and the group stoned it dead. Police fire stopped just as suddenly. A kid and a man lay dead, with several others wounded.

It seemed everybody was terribly shaken, but much more so, the pupils themselves. They were baffled, sullen, and grim. They had not, it seemed, expected it. Dumb-struck, they stood in groups all over the area while the wounded lay groaning on the ground. And for a moment even the on-lookers, who had watched the singing and placard-waving and then the bloody spectacle, seemed petrified with fright. The peaceful protest march had turned sour in a devastatingly cruel sort of way, an unprovoked show of power.

While the children stood, almost in a trance, police climbed onto their vehicles. They drove away and camped on an open ground across Klip River which runs between Orlando East and Orlando West townships. For a while, the scattered and bewildered pupils remained immobile. Then they regrouped, returning to the street. Helped by motorists and reporters, they collected the dead and the wounded. Some were driven to Baragwanath Hospital about two miles away, some were carried to the nearby Phefeni Clinic.

In the confusion, an African policeman was cornered by pupils in a toilet at a house near the scene. He was beaten, then handcuffed with his own handcuffs and chased down the street across the river. A shyish teenage schoolgirl, Antoinette Pieterson, was searching in the confusion for her young brother, Hector. She had seen him in the crowds earlier that morning and told him not to disappear for she wanted to go home with him after the march.

Now Hector, twelve years old and a standard four pupil, had melted away. Where could he be? Had he fled home, leaving her behind? She wondered as she mingled with the milling thousands. He had left home in Jabavu, where they attended school and lived with grandma Martha Tolk, the day before. He had spent the night with their parents in Meadowlands and joined the protest march without going home to Jabavu that morning. She wanted him to go home with her. Where could he be? Then Tiny, as Antoinette was also called, saw a group of boys surrounding a youngster who lay injured on the side of a street. She went to them. As she could not clearly see the kid lying on the ground, she moved closer and looked. Hector! It was Hector; he was bleeding. He had been shot. She called him. He neither responded nor opened his eyes. She screamed hysterically. Someone, tall and wearing tattered, sullied overalls, helped Tiny carry the injured lad away. The tall boy carried him in his arms.

She was in her school uniform, walking on the side. The horror of the whole tragedy was mirrored in their faces as they walked down the street. They took him to the clinic. Here, the nurses asked them to wait while they took the injured boy to a doctor in another room. She waited. The big boy left. Hector was certified dead, but Tiny was not told. Instead, the nurse told women teachers who were also at the clinic, and the teachers asked her to take them to her home, where they broke the bad news to the family.

Wearing white shorts and a white jacket, Dr Nthato Motlana, deputy chairman of the Parents Vigilante Committee, trotted past a group of pupils down Vilakazi Street. He stopped in front of the house of Dr Matlhare, where another group stood chattering. Visibly shaken, Motlana muttered: 'It's bad, terribly bad.' He wanted to see Matlhare. But Matlhare, he was told, was not around. He had taken some of the wounded to the hospital.

The Parents Vigilante Committee, said Motlana while waiting, was responsible for the ugliness which had happened. If Dr Sipho

Nyembezi, its chairman, had called a meeting as he had repeatedly asked him to do, they could have avoided the whole bloody mess by negotiating with the Department of Bantu Education to rescind its Afrikaans order.

A teetotaller and non-smoker, Motlana had, since the banning of the ANC, devoted his life to serving the Soweto community. He had founded the Black Medical Discussion Group in the 1960s to raise funds from its members to help needy medical students.

Modest, despite his success as a medical practitioner with other business interests, he was involved in many other community organisations. He had helped form the vigilante committee during the 1972 university student disturbances. The committee had negotiated re-admission of expelled students with some measure of success. Characteristically, he seemed utterly concerned today. Though highly respected in the community even by the Black Consciousness leadership, he was often criticised in private for not throwing in his lot with the BPC.

He was still talking when he saw Matlhare among another group a distance away. He ran to him. After their talk he whispered to me that his committee would be joining hands with the Soweto Parents Association, which was headed by Matlhare, in order to speak in one voice and plan a mass funeral for the dead. The vigilante committee executive would meet that evening, he said. He would tell other members of the new plan. The Soweto Parents Association would also meet. He and Matlhare would confer by telephone after the meetings.

Vastly different from Motlana in character, though equally tiny, Matlhare was bashful, soft-spoken and loved good, expensive clothes. He was almost always nattily dressed and until fairly recently had never shown interest in public affairs. He had in fact become involved by accident. His daughter and nine other pupils from Naledi High School died in a bus crash while on holiday in Mozambique in 1974. A disaster fund committee was elected to handle monies raised from the general public to help bereaved families. When the fund committee failed to assist families despite the fact that more than R10 000 had been collected, Matlare intervened in an attempt to bring about justice. And it was during those protracted attempts that the Soweto Parents Association was born, with him as interim chairman.

As he went away, Matlhare asked me to attend his executive committee meeting in his surgery that evening. He had, he said, not been to work since early that morning. It was obvious a merger was on the cards; the evening meetings were mere formalities.

A pall of smoke was billowing in Pela Street, not far from the scene of the shootings. A band of pupils was burning a municipal vehicle while thousands more roamed Pela and Vilakazi Streets. They were putting up roadblocks with derelict cars from the side of the streets.

In Vilakazi Street, a group of students attacked a milk delivery truck. As the driver fled, pupils grabbed the milk before driving the vehicle away. With it, they conveyed others to strategic points within the townships for more roadblocks. Another vehicle, a company car, was set alight: a trailer sped recklessly down the streets amid shouts of 'Amandla! Amandla!' It was driven by some students. A helicopter hovered above, dropping teargas on the crowds milling within the streets. Vehicles were being stoned in Pela Street, the main road from Phefeni to Johannesburg.

Rioting erupted. Confusion reigned everywhere. Police remained across the river, with more re-enforcements from the riot squad joining them.

At Central West Jabavu, just below Morris Isaacson High School, a mob of angry children attacked the administration offices after they chased a white man into the building. They smashed windows. They dragged Dr Melville Edelstein, a social welfare officer, out and stoned him dead; the building was gutted. Black workers watched in horror as children, using rocks, crushed his head.

It was quite apparent that school children directed their venom at police, whites, commercial vehicles, administration buildings and virtually everything connected with the government. To them, everything connected with or symbolising authority had to be destroyed. Blacks who would not respond to the rallying cry by raising a clenched fist and shouting, when the kids screamed the same cry and saluted, were also beaten. They had their private personal vehicles damaged too.

A raised clenched fist, the Black Power salute, had become a passport to safety.

Something was burning in a street above. We could only see dark smoke billowing in the air. I ran up the road to see what it was.

'Get back,' a band of students some distance away shouted. I stopped almost instantly, looking at them. They waved at me to get back. There was no other way. Defiance would spell trouble, I thought. As I retreated I had a brainwave. Glancing to see whether they watched, I jumped into the yard, then into another, joining an elderly woman. 'Oh, our children, what are they doing?' she shook her head in disbelief. A van belonging to West Rand Administration Board (WRAB), the notorious regional authority governing Soweto, was on fire. Pupils had set it alight. She did not know what had happened to the poor driver. He must have escaped, she said somewhat wistfully. She seemed stricken with fear, fear of what might happen as a result of what was happening, I thought. I wondered whether she blamed the children or the police for what was happening. 'P-o-w-e-r!' shrill voices pierced the air for the umpteenth time. I got back, waited outside. I went into the house of Dr Matlhare.

I was still phoning inside the house, talking to the news desk at the office, when the servant banged the door, shouting. 'Come out; they will kill us. They are burning the house,' she screamed plaintively. Without thinking, I also shouted into the telephone: 'I'm phoning from Dr Matlhare's house. They are burning the house.' I hung up, running behind the servant, out of the house.

A mob of youngsters lingered in front of the house. 'It is his car,' the servant mumbled, pointing at me. And the mob surrounded me. 'Is that your car?' some shouted, pointing at a Volkswagen parked near the motor-gate.

'No, it's not mine. It belongs to *The World* newspaper and I work for the *The Star.*'

'It's a lie. We're burning it if it's not yours. Can we?'

'If you want you can burn it. It's not mine.'

'It belongs to the police, we understand.'

'You can burn it if you want, but it isn't a police car; it belongs to *The World.*'

They looked at one another.

'Los hom – leave him,' someone said.

'Okay, Daddy,' they scuttled away in a pack.

A little later, however, someone came to fetch the car. It was not a member of *The World* staff! Had I mistakenly saved a police vehicle? I felt ill at ease.

Sis Winnie drove up Vilakazi Street, returning home from work. She was the same as ever, slender and beautiful. She had heard of the shooting and rioting while at work in the city. She had come back to see what was happening. She parked her car outside the garage at the back of her house, which was surrounded by a high concrete wall. Her Alsatian dog, chained a little away from the back door, barked endlessly. Inside the yard, five school girls in gym-dresses sat talking in whispers. She entered the house through the back door without greeting the girls who huddled in a corner of the yard. No one, it seemed, was inside the house. She came out in no time. She raised her hand, only then greeting the children.

We climbed into her car. Had I been to Baragwanath Hospital. How many children had been killed? She questioned me as she reversed the vehicle and drove up the road. A woman of boundless courage and a tough, uncompromising political campaigner, Sis Winnie was serious but calm. She looked straight ahead and did not respond to the shouts from the kids manning roadblocks. She turned right at the scene of the shooting that had sparked the riot. She drove towards the main Pela Street. Bands of screaming children roamed the street. The main road teemed with thousands of people, young and old. They watched several vehicles burning along the street. After crossing the main road, we swung round and parked. A large crowd crammed the area above us and opposite the clinic. A helicopter roared in the air from the direction of Orlando East towards us. It circled above the crowded spot ahead. Police vans from across the rivulet below began moving in convoy up Pela Street. A number of children scattered in all directions. Sis Winnie wished she had a loud-hailer. She would, she said, tell them not to wander about but to remain in one place. She feared police would pick and shoot them with ease if they moved about singly. At least they would be hesitant, she said, to open fire if people stood in one place because they knew some people would talk publicity about their behaviour.

She asked a group of boys standing next to us to tell other children not to move. They looked at her, but did nothing. The police convoys stopped in a side street near the clinic along the main road and the helicopter above kept its protective watch. More people rushed to the spot. Winnie and I walked up too.

An ambulance pulled up. It stopped in the middle of the road directly opposite the side street. Police surrounded the ambulance. Two whites took out a stretcher from the ambulance. They went into the street. They collected the burnt body of an employee of WRAB, a white official, from the right side of the pavement. On the left, a van was smouldering. Some said it belonged to the dead man.

The ambulance, closely followed by the police convoy, drove off in the direction of Orlando Police Station across the river. The crowds sauntered away. We, too, left. Sis Winnie wanted me to take her later that evening to the executive meeting of the Soweto Parents Association in Naledi. She would return home with Matlhare after the meeting, she said. As sunset approached, rioting increased in intensity and ferocity. Smoke from burning buildings and vehicles obscured the heavens above. Like a cloud, it hung darkly over the settlement. Below, vehicles and government buildings smouldered. Bands of chanting youths, armed with home-made petrol bombs, roamed the streets. Thousands of workers were streaming back home. They alighted from trains, buses and taxis and found youths milling through the streets and the township burning. Press photographer Len Khumalo was caught up in the rumpus. He was accosted by a group after a schoolgirl had seen him attempting to take a picture. His cameras were smashed and his life threatened because, they said, he was a sell-out. Cold with fright, young Khumalo pleaded for mercy.

If you are a brother, prove it,' they shouted as they dragged him. 'Smash this building,' a young man, pointing at a government building, shoved a stone into his hand.' We are going to break it down; you must throw the first stone.' Trembling, he looked at the building, he then closed his eyes, hurling the stone. A window shattered amid cries of 'Amandla'. They attacked the administration building and it was ablaze in no time. They had petrol, Khumalo thought. He noticed some of the children were keeping an eye on him. He was too scared to ask them to let him go.

Like so many others, Khumalo had been unlucky. He had arrived in the township late but immediately got into trouble. From the burning building, the rioters ordered him to go with them to Phomolong. Several other youngsters joined them along the way as they marched, singing and shouting towards Phomolong rail station. Somehow, he felt a little calm. They would not kill him, after all. If they spared his life, he reckoned, he could always buy other cameras.

The mobsters stormed into Phomolong beerhall. They hurled insults at the old people drinking inside. Liquor, they shouted at the guzzlers, made it impossible for them to fight for their land, their freedom. Some scuttled out as the youngsters turned things upside down; others joined the kids. The nearby bottle store was burgled and looted. 'Take, brother. You'll quench your thirst when you get home,' a kid handed Khumalo a half-dozen beers. A teetotaller, he grabbed the loot all the same without much ado. But it was not until much later that he managed to escape under cover of darkness. The experience had been so shattering, he said, that the thought of police apprehension never struck him as they plundered the township administration offices and liquor stores.

Meanwhile in Naledi, Johannes Kgari had joined some people in a neighbour's house drinking the spoils grabbed from the local bottle store. They talked of the looting and the shooting. Everybody was helping himself at the bottle store and they too had taken the stuff on the table before them. A bachelor, Kgari had arrived home earlier than usual. It was still quiet when he reached home. He left his place of work in the city early because he feared he might find himself in trouble if he returned late. On arrival he had gone to a cousin's house in another section of the township. While on the way there he had seen a crowd of pupils attacking a bus at the corner of Legwale and Ntswe streets. The children stoned it as it sped past on the way to Zola. It seemed the driver was on the run for there were no passengers in the bus. It was his first sight of real action. And as he walked on he heard loud noises further down. He could hear the shouting, but not what was said. The noises came from Emndeni and seemed from a picnic.

They cleaned the table. Kgari and two other men stood up. They went out into the street and walked up to Naledi Bottle Store. Along the way, they met groups and groups of people carrying liquor. Some carried the bottles by hand, some in cartons and paper bags. 'This is our money, how long has the white man been robbing us,' an old man said and laughed. The bottle store was jammed with looters. Kgari and his acquaintances could hardly get close, let alone gain entry. They waited at a distance. The two chaps melted away into the crowds. He remained standing on the pavement wondering what to do.

A car pulled to the side. Inside were five students. They greeted him. He knew only one of them. They were going to Mapetla, they told him. He climbed into the car without even finding out what they were going to do there. They drove along Mphatlalatsane Street towards Merafe railway station. The street was filled with people, young and old, cavorting. 'The pigs have killed our brothers. We'll show them something today,' said one of the gang in the car.

Another crowd hung around Merafe Bottle Store. People were looting the store too. Some youngsters emerged from the crowd and gave them bottles of brandy and beers, then they disappeared. They drove on and finally stopped outside the Mapetla Hostel, where there was yet another crowd. No sooner had they got there than another car, also filled with schoolboys, joined them. Some of the boys who were with him went out to the other party in the other vehicle. Together they walked to the hostel gate. Some hostel–dwellers were standing there. It seemed they had been waiting for the schoolboys.

The nearby bottle store was being looted, but the beerhall adjacent to the superintendent's office was burning. The two cars moved away one after the other. They went to Moletsane beerhall and bar lounge. They too were looted and burnt. Some of the children wanted to burn the Entokozweni Early Learning Centre nearby, some felt it shouldn't be. An argument ensued.

A giant institution in the life of the townships, Entokozweni had been erected by Van Leer, a Dutch company with international interests. It was a nursery school with a difference. Here, unlike elsewhere in the ghetto, the black child was not only looked after while his parents were at work; he was also a subject for study to see how the environment affected his general development, influenced his behavior. Teams of medical practitioners and trained social workers were at his disposal. Great care was taken, too, over his feeding and pre-school education. For both young and old, the institution was also a recreation centre. Here they played indoor games, held social parties, learnt cooking, knitting and sewing among other things.

'Come on,' one of students said. 'It's another symbol of oppression. It must go.'

'But tell me, who suffers if we destroy it?' another cried.

'Is it not a symbol of oppression?'

'It may be, but...'

'Then we break it down too.'

'Well, we must burn all the houses in Soweto thereafter.'

'What do you mean?'

'They are also symbols of oppression, aren't they?'

The boys finally agreed that the centre benefited the community and that destroying it would hurt residents. They left it intact and so too the Tladi Clinic down below. Thereafter, they attacked the Urban Bantu Council Chamber, but their efforts failed miserably. Only the front windows of that concrete massive structure were smashed. At best a tourist attraction, the council chamber had been established in 1968 to serve as a parliament of sorts in the context of the peculiarly South African concept of separate freedoms. It was, in essence, a ploy to fool urban blacks to believe they were being given some sort of political dispensation. But Soweto children and the majority of their parents were never fooled. If anything, it seemed, the government succeeded in fooling itself.

By 3am the students were attempting to burn Naledi Hall but seemed to have run out of petrol. Kgari, drunk, felt tired. He had been swept up by the mood of the day before. All he wanted was a complete rest, to get away from it all. Quietly, he slipped away.

The morning was more frightening than even the shootings had been the day before. Soweto was utterly on the binge now with residents, most of them young, staggering up and down the streets, still looting bottle stores and cars indiscriminately. I felt dead scared and had a nagging feeling that police would wipe us off to the last man.

The executive meeting of the Soweto Parents Association had not taken place. Matlhare himself had been trapped in his surgery, unable to venture out, until after midnight.

Lots and lots of properties had been pillaged during the night. Damage included more than hundred administration offices, ninety-four liquor outlets, fifty Putco buses, more than two hundred vehicles and a multitude of houses in which buses had crashed as drivers fled from attackers. Hundreds of people were missing too. They had failed to reach home the night before and nobody knew whether they had been killed or arrested. Ariel Thabo Kgongoane, a Kaizer Chiefs soccer star, lay dead in his car across Klip River on the old Potchefstroom Road, just a stone's throw from the Chinese business complex at the bottom of Rockville. He had been shot dead by police while allegedly running away with his loot from the shops. The car was partially submerged in the river.

But it was not until later that day, after Prime Minister John Vorster speaking before Parliament, told the nation over the air that law and order would be maintained at all costs, that hell broke loose. Police, who had shown a little restrain all along, threw all caution to the wind. By the end of the day sixty-five black people were dead, sixty-two of them shot by police. Forty-eight were adults, eight were youths and six were children.

CHAPTER 4

AT VARIANCE

Situated rather elegantly on a rocky hillside surrounded by dry open cactus country, Turfloop University had awakened to a shrill passionate chant. Students, nearly a thousand of them, sang the African national anthem. The rest of the community was taken aback. They could clearly hear the spirited chant as they prepared themselves to get to work. By night while they slept, the student body had resolved to demonstrate their solidarity with Soweto. And they had heatedly argued until midnight on how to show their support. Some had wanted to demonstrate on the main Pietersburg/Tzaneen road outside the university campus and to harass white motorists travelling on the road. Some felt that would be dangerous as it would expose them to the police who, they said, were bound to come eventually. Then the students had dispersed after agreeing to hold a prayer demonstration on the university sports field. They would also not go to lectures that day, they decided.

The students had initially met inside the hall to look into the question of establishing a Students Representative Council which was disbanded after the 1972 disturbances. Recent attempts to revive the council had failed because the university administration had tried to impose its stooges on students. However, a committee had eventually been formed, with blessings from the administration, specifically to form a new SRC. But no sooner had they met in the hall than they shelved the SRC issue and raised the events in Soweto.

Since daybreak they had been trickling onto the sports field, bringing with them posters that condemned apartheid generally, and in particular expressed sympathy with the victims of police brutality in Soweto. A few, apparently those who did not want to participate or were simply too concerned with impending half-year examinations, had stayed in their dormitories. But the more dedicated had turned up.

Soon staff, black and white, came out on to the campus. Dumbstruk, they stood in front of the administration block. They watched the amassed students below. No one dared to go near. The singing continued. Then the students, tense and shouting slogans, suddenly broke into two groups. One column marched northwards towards the girl's hostels, then right towards the administration block; the other moved south-eastwards, then turned left towards the administration block too. The columns approached each other. But they turned west just as they were about to meet and marched side by side past the recreation hall back to sports field. They stopped singing and, silently, prayed before reading poetry and resumed singing freedom songs.

Police, armed with rifles and accompanied by dogs, arrived. They stood and watched from a distance. Smoke billowed from the recreation hall. Someone had set the hall alight. The police charged and the demonstrators ran in all directions. Several students were beaten. A final year Bachelor of Science student from Klerksdorp later died in hospital. That morning a library was gutted at the University of Zululand. In Alexandra, north of Johannesburg, school children, armed with stones and using dustbin lids for shields, fought gun-toting police. The uprising had spread to other areas: to Lebowa, KwaZulu, and Bophuthatswana homelands as well as to Kagiso, Vosloorus and Thembisa townships in the Witwatersrand.

Whatever police restraint had existed the day before was now abandoned. Police were shooting, arresting people at random.

Residents were simply stunned by the ruthlessness meted out against them. But whatever doubts they still had about the behaviour of the police were soon dispelled. Resolute and unyielding, Prime Minister John Vorster, talking over the air, said he had ordered police to use all the means at their disposal without fear or favour to protect life and property. They had been ordered to maintain law and order at all costs. There was no reason for panic, he said, because police were doing their duty. His government would not be intimidated. Order within the country was more important to him. The reason for the unrest was to create large scale panic, he said.

In Soweto, the Black Community Programme (BCP) was busy planning a meeting for Sunday, 20 June at the African Methodist Episcopal Church, Dube Village, to discuss police brutality. However, when residents pitched up at the church at 2pm they found a government notice pinned on the door. Jimmy Kruger, the Minister of Justice and Police, had banned the meeting. Not only had he banned the gathering, but he had also ordered his men to make sure his order was obeyed. They stood by. Residents insisted that the meeting should go on regardless. But organisers persuaded them to leave, after they had successfully appealed to the police to go, if only temporarily.

At sunset I called at the Mandela household to tell Sis Winnie why I had failed to pick her up for the executive meeting of Soweto Parents Association on Wednesday evening. She seemed to have known the meeting had not taken place. A meeting was to be held shortly, she said. I could attend if I wanted. She disappeared into an inner room. I sat in the lounge. BPC's national president, Kenneth Rachidi, arrived. With him was Tom Manthata, a BPC executive member, and Aubrey Mokoena, fieldworker for the Black Community Programmes, as well as student leaders Tsietsi Mashinini, Tebello Motapanyane, Zweli Sizani and Seth Mazibuko. They joined me in the lounge.

Sis Winnie returned. Matlhare, she said, did not want the meeting to be held at his house. She neither knew his reason nor did she mind if they met in her home. Visibly apprehensive, Seth, a sixteen-year-old, loudly wondered if there was no other place. Someone suggested a check be made at Fr Desmond Tutu's house. Mokoena went out to the Dean's house down the road. The young student leaders preferred the meeting to be held elsewhere. They suspected the Mandela household was under police surveillance. Nobody could tell whether their suspicions were groundless or not. Winnie had always been a target for cops. When Mokoena returned we trooped to the Dean's house where we found Motlana and Matlhare already waiting. With them was the Dean himself.

But as we settled down, Fr Tutu rose. Be at home, he said. He could not be with us because he had an engagement elsewhere. He was, he said jokingly, a mere minister of religion, not a politician. We laughed. Winnie said the Dean should not be allowed to go to Lesotho (Tutu had just been appointed bishop for the former British protectorate). Soweto needed him, she said. Furrowing his forehead, Tutu stared at her, winked, before stepping out into the corridor without a word.

Without any further ado, the meeting opened with a prayer by Tsietsi, the freckle-faced nineteen-year-old from Morrison Isaacson High. He was brief, impressively brief, confident and forthright in his prayer. There was no agenda. Motlana read a statement which, he said, he had prepared. He wished the gathering to adopt it as its resolution. The statement that condemned police action against defenceless, innocent children was accepted only after additions were made on it. Mokoena was entrusted with seeing to its publication in newspapers. Then it was decided that a bigger and more representative meeting of relevant organisations be called soon to plan a mass funeral of victims of the shootings. Neither the venue nor date of the proposed meeting was decided.

Tebello, a rather roly-poly, gangling chappie, accused *The Star* of having published a story the day before the student march giving details of the route they would follow. That story, he claimed, had brought the police to the demonstration.

An outrageous lie, I thought.

Tsietsi, Seth and Zweli shook their heads.

'Maybe Harry can tell us who wrote the report,' Motlana said.

'I did but…'

'*Awo!*' They chorused, exchanging glances.

'Gentlemen, if you're going to lead the people you have to be honest and truthful,' I said as politely as I could. 'The story I wrote which was published by the newspaper contained none of these allegations. I can bring a cutting for proof.'

They listened intently. I shifted in my seat.

'You'll remember,' I said looking at Tebello, 'I asked you when students at Naledi began the march to tell me where they were going. Would I have asked you if I knew where they were going and their route?'

'Who told you students were going to hold a demonstration?' someone, I think it was Tsietsi, asked.

'Mr. Mathabathe.'

'Did he say you should publish the story?'

'No, he merely said some of his students had told him there would be a demonstration. I wrote and published the story because I believed it was in the public interest.'

Silence.

It struck me that the accusation was not so much directed at the newspaper as at me. Tebello was challenging my presence, I thought. I feared I would be thrown out. However, sanity prevailed.

Matlhare said he had encountered a great difficulty taking the injured from the scene to hospital. Police were not co-operative at all. In fact they went out of their way to interfere with him. He was still talking when Sis Winnie, staring at Motlana, interrupted.

'You, what role did you play?'

'Who, me? What do you mean?' Motlana, startled, asked.

Silence fell over the room again. Sis Winnie, who sat directly opposite the two medical doctors, quickly turned her head, glancing at Tebello. 'He refused to carry the injured because he said he was afraid his car would get dented,' Tebello blurted out. Motlana was outraged.

'Are you trying to say that I, a medical doctor, refused to help the injured because I did not want to see my car damaged? Rubbish, what's a car to me. I can't take this shit, man,' he said.

Sis Winnie grinned.

Matlhare muttered something in protest. Tebello tried to explain where and when the doctor had refused to help, but Motlana was too angry to allow that. He kept on shouting, 'Shit, I can't stand this shit.'

Shaking his head in apparent disbelief, Motlana rose. He stormed out of the hushed room. Someone, I think it was Mokoena, ran after him and brought him back. Matlhare, Rachidi and Manthata told Tebello to withdraw his allegations unreservedly. Reluctantly, he yielded. 'I withdraw all I said,' he said, extending his hand to Motlana. They shook hands.

An uneasy calm settled over the room. They tried to continue talking, but it was apparent that that was no longer possible. The atmosphere was simply too tense, too charged. The meeting closed, rather unceremoniously.

The student leaders were an unknown quantity before the uprising. Soweto, let alone the country, had never heard of them. Even Sasm, the high school organisation, was relatively unknown. It had never been publicly involved in any issue affecting the community. But overnight they had become too powerful. At 8pm the next evening the bigger, more representative meeting was held at the Methodist Church Youth Centre in Central West Jabavu. In attendance were representatives of Saso, BPC, Soweto Parent

Association, Black Community Programmes, Black Social Workers Association, Sasm, Post-primary Principals' Union and the Institute of Black Studies. In the chair sat Dr Matlhare, assisted by Dr Manas Buthelezi, a Lutheran theologian. Word of support came from the Interdenominational African Minister Association of SA (IDAMASA), Young Women's Christian Association, and the National Federation of Women, whose representatives could not, for various reasons, be present. The name Soweto Parents Association was dropped in favour of Black Parents Association. Motlana argued that the original name was too narrow, exclusive. People in other townships, he said, would consider its activities as being confined to Soweto whereas the uprising had spread to other areas. What was wanted was a broad, more accommodating name. Sis Winnie shared his view. As the association would be planning a mass funeral of the victims and giving financial relief to bereaved families, it was necessary, she said, to change the name so that no area could be left out. She also suggested that people in areas such as Alexandra should be encouraged to form branches of the association and be promised financial aid, if enough funds were raised. Buthelezi was elected chairman and Matlhare his deputy. Mokoena became first secretary and Ben Nteso, the president of the Social Workers Association, second secretary. Buthelezi, Matlhare and Motlana were also elected trustees of the association. Winnie was among other executive committee members.

A fund was immediately launched when Saso and BPC contributed R200 each and Matlhare handed in R100 from the now defunct Soweto Parent Association. It was also agreed that the Black Parents Association (BPA) should discourage any other organisation or group of individuals from raising money from public for the same purpose. The young student leaders expressed concern and unhappiness that school principals had earlier that day decided to raise funds from pupils for the burial of the dead. They claimed that some principals would misuse the contributions.

Although the scholars were persuaded to change their attitude – it was argued that principals held responsible positions within the community and would give collection to the fund – they never contributed anything. Apparently because their leaders were not satisfied with the arrangement they wanted to collect money from pupils themselves, without interference from principles. Buthelezi, a keen exponent of black theology within Black Consciousness philosophy, was a relative newcomer to Soweto, but a highly respected theologian known virtually throughout the country. A former regional director of the Christian Institute in Natal, he had studied at Yale University for an MA degree in Sacred Theology, briefly lectured at Washington University in the United States and also at Heidelberg University in West Germany. He was banned by the government in December 1973, but unbanned in May the following year. To him, the BPA represented, for the first time since the ANC and PAC were outlawed, a united front of organisations that did not necessarily have the same beliefs, a development that symbolised black unity and which could not be ignored even by people disinterested in progress among blacks. His secretary Mokoena, born and bred within the ghetto, was not only a deeply committed Christian, but had long been involved in the Black Consciousness movement, promoting it in the community. A Saso devotee of long standing, Mokoena was detained by the security police in 1974 after the 'Viva Frelimo' rally, but later released without any charges having been laid against him. After his expulsion from Turfloop University in 1972, he studied and completed a BA degree through the University of South Africa.

Several meetings of the association were later held at Buthelezi's home in Dube Village, planning the mass funeral. An application for permission to hold the burial was made to the Johannesburg chief magistrate while attempts to list all the dead were made. Bereaved families were told, in the meantime, not to worry about funeral arrangements. The association considered them its responsibility.

However, the first stumbling block came when the association discovered, much to its dismay, that police were not only unwilling to co-operate, but actually tried to stop the bereaved families giving bodies to the association. Security police also began visiting Matlhare and Sis Winnie in an apparent move to intimidate the association.

Matlhare said they had called on him three times but did not find him home each time. They had left messages for him to see them at John Vorster Square, their headquarters. However, Soweto parents rallied behind the association in spite of police harassment. Some of the dead could not be found anywhere nor could police say what happened to them. Many parents claimed in reports to the association and the press that relatives were missing. But it was difficult to determine whether the missing persons had died or had been arrested because of the attitude of the police. Rumours were rife too that some of the dead had been secretly buried within the premises of some police stations. Official figures of the dead were disputed by people who claimed the figures were deliberately intended to bluff the nation and the outside world.

Whatever tenuous accord existed between the old guard BPA leadership and the young student leadership was threatened when Jimmy Kruger, the all-powerful Minister of Police, banned the planned mass burial at the end of June. He announced over the radio that permission could not be granted because, he said, it was known that black power organisations were behind the move to hold the service. The chief magistrate had sent the application to Kruger after Buthelezi had refused to hand in to him a list of all the people who would speak at the service and their written speeches. Buthelezi had explained that that was impossible for him to do as the service was a church affair and many priests from difference churches would participate.

Now Buthelezi, looking weary, claimed there was nothing more the association could do. It was clear that the spectre of what had happened after BPC and Saso defied Kruger's ban over the 'Viva Frelimo' rally hung over their heads. Buthelezi did not, he said, want to bring trouble to a lot of innocent people. He believed every one of the dead victims belonged to a church and that families would, therefore, not find it difficult to get a pastor to perform each burial service.

Zweli, one of the student leaders, angrily told the tiny gathering inside Buthelezi's house that it was completely wrong to capitulate. He himself, he said, had been doing rounds on behalf of the association, telling bereaved families the association would bury the dead. He had arranged with the Soweto Taxi Association to provide free transport for mourners to get to the cemetery. Was he now expected to go back to the families and the taxi association to tell them that they were no longer burying the dead? That was something, he said, he could never do. And he believed if the association had been serious right from the beginning, it should hold the service as planned despite the Minister's utterances. Sis Winnie, agreeing with him, accused the chairman of being cowardly. The association, she said, had committed itself. It also had an image to uphold and could not tell the people to go it alone. What would the people of Soweto, if not the entire black community throughout the country, think of the association and of them as leaders? It was the association's responsibility to bury the dead. It should do so regardless of the ban, no matter the consequences.

'I am not prepared to do that,' Buthelezi groaned, interrupting Sis Winnie. Mokoena reiterated Zweli's and Sis Winnie's sentiments. Buthelezi seemed totally restless. He also appeared to have made up his mind to resign rather than defy the Minister's ban.

Somehow Motlana, who had so far listened quietly, but with a worried look on his face, came to the rescue. It would be wrong, he said, to try to completely overlook the Minister's refusal to give permission; that would only place some people in danger. Avoiding unnecessary trouble was not cowardice, but a sign of being responsible. He agreed, he said, the association had an image to uphold and also that it would be terrible for it to withdraw. He believed, however, that the best way out was a compromise. He suggested that the association should go ahead with at least one massive burial service to symbolise all the dead. The symbolic funeral service could be conducted on Hector Pieterson.

Motlana's suggestion brought a sigh of relief to the chairman. Also, to second secretary Nteso, who had seemed lost in despair. Sis Winnie, Zweli and Mokoena were visibly unimpressed.

But then Zweli was not a member of the executive. The chairman, after whispering to Motlana, ruled that non-executive members should leave the room to give the committee a chance to finalise the matter. Matlhare had not come to the meeting. Shaking his head, Zweli and a few other people, who had been listening, shuffled out of the room into the kitchen. They closed the door behind them.

Buthelezi said Motlana's suggestion was wise. It had to be accepted. Nteso endorsed the suggestion. Apparently realising they could not win if the matter was put to a vote, Winnie and Mokoena remained silent. The suggestion was accepted without any further wrangling. The symbolic funeral of Hector, reputed to have been the first victim, was to be held on Saturday, 3 July, the day originally chosen for the proposed mass burial.

'We made a terrible mistake,' Zweli remarked at the end of the meeting, 'thinking we could work with these old men. They are co-operating with the system.'

The heat was on soon after the symbolic funeral. Security police stepped up their activities in Soweto. Seth, Zweli and David Kutumela, another schoolboy, as well as Manthata, were the first causalities. They were detained. Other student leaders Tsietsi and Tebello, and also Mokoena, went into hiding. Matlhare soon became bedridden. A week-long conference, organised by the Institute of Black Studies, which was a founder member of BPC, was banned. The conference, organised by Nimrod Mkele, director of the Institute, was intended for blacks to take a deep look into their condition and make proposals for the future. Kruger did not want the conference to be held in Soweto where, he claimed, it would inflame tempers. Meanwhile his men harassed Nim, as Mkele was popularly known. They demanded from him all the speeches of the people he had invited to give talks at the conference. A tall, scholarly man who held an MA degree in industrial psychology, Nim had spent money and time for a year interesting people in the Institute, drawing up its draft constitution and finally planning the inaugural conference. And there had been no secrecy whatsoever over what he was doing. The press had given it ample coverage which meant that most people knew for weeks, if not months, before June 16 that his conference was scheduled to take place in Soweto. It was now banned exactly a day before opening and had to be held elsewhere, if at all.

Kutumela was released from detention after a week or two. Tsietsi and other student leaders still outside began talking of planning a protest march into Johannesburg, the citadel of white economic power, to demand the release of Zweli and Seth in particular. The kids seemed just as determined and undeterred as John Vorster himself. He wanted law and order maintained at any cost; they wanted him to release their colleagues, no matter the consequences.

CHAPTER 5

A HARVEST OF DESPAIR

Nimrod Mkele moved backwards and forwards, like a madman, receiving his guest speakers and making last minute arrangements for the inaugural conference which had been banned from the Young Christian Women's Association hall in Dube Village, Soweto. He could not possibly cancel the conference. Many of the speakers had already arrived. Some had come all the way from the United States, while others were still arriving from cities like Gaborone, Maseru, Cape Town and Durban.

But there was also fear that some might decide not to turn up after reading press reports that the conference had been banned. Time was against him. He didn't quite know himself whether or not the conference would really take off, though he wished and hoped it would.

His office in Braamfontein, Johannesburg and his home in Zola, Soweto had been searched, apparently because the security police did not believe that advance copies of papers to be delivered at the conference had not been sent in. It seemed even to close friends that all his efforts of almost twelve months had been in vain. However, affable Nim went on as usual – cheerful and full of laughter – with plans in spite of the ban and raids.

Dutifully his secretary, Cecilia Palmer, held the fort at their office. She answered calls from journalists and interested persons, who were anxious to know what was happening. But all she could say was that her boss was still hunting for a new venue. And she felt pretty jumpy each time there was a knock at the door. Was it another visit from the cops?

I called in on her at about 5pm on Tuesday, 13 July, the day the conference should have opened in Soweto. Nim had arranged to hold the conference at Wilgespruit. He had spent most of his time out of the office that day, but had instructed his secretary to take some guests, due at any time from Cape Town, to Wilgespruit. She was still waiting for them. A photostat machine, an electric typewriter and stack upon stack of plain sheets of paper, as well as numerous records related to the conference, had to be transferred to the new venue too. The conference would officially open that night, but nothing much was expected to happen. Nim would be there. There would be some drinks, a party. Would I attend the opening, she wanted to know. Unlikely, I said. Tomorrow, yes.

Wilgespruit lay in a gorge north of Roodepoort. It comprised a sprinkling of brick and stone-walled cottages in the woods on the side of one of three steep mountains. With a parking lot, telephone, private rooms, offices, hall, kitchen for mass cooking, toilet facilities, lawns and electricity, it was self-sufficient.

To get there from Soweto, you drove through Dobsonville past some farms, mine dumps and turned left into Main Reef Road immediately after crossing a railway line, then right into and through Roodepoort until you reached Ontdekkers Road up the hill. Then you turned left again and drove along the road. You passed several cafés, garages, houses and flats on the side of the road. At the robots opposite Horison shopping centre, you turned right into a smaller street and for minutes drove though another residential area.

Soon after driving past a large church building on the right, you turned left and headed straight into a forest. A dirt road meandered sharply past rocks and tall trees. Even the soil seemed different; it was loose, soft, despite the rocks and tall grass on the roadside. You descended all the time and the descent was steep; so much so that you felt as if you were entering the bowels of the very earth itself.

Wooded mountains stood on either side and ahead. And you loved it, to no end.

Looking from the parking lot down the unfolding valley you saw several assorted homesteads with tiled roofs on the vast farmlands in the distance beyond the tall bluegum trees, protea and cactus shrubs around you. Some of the farms were red; they had been ploughed. But others were still grey with dry grass. A tarred road, seemingly from nowhere, cut across in the distance below and girded, as it were, the two mountains standing face to face. What a spectacle! What beauty!

A cross was perched high up on the crown of the mountain on the east side; two foot paths wound from the base below. And they met at the foot of the cross. The mountain on the south side seemed as if it were the head and body of Wilgespruit, while the two others (one on the west side and one on the east), her outstretched limbs. People trickled daily into Wilgespruit. Most were young, but the Soweto student leaders were not among them. They must have feared that security police or their informers would be around and follow them to their hide-outs at the end of the conference. However, some arrived each morning, had meals in between sessions and returned 'home' late in the evening when the workday ended. Those people who came from afar and had no relations in Johannesburg stayed at the centre each night.

Throughout the conference the black people's experience came under the microscope, as speakers took a look into their condition through the history of South Africa. Segregation had always been their lot, even before the advent of National Party rule in 1948.

Fatima Meer, a noted sociologist from Natal, was making a subtle distinction between segregation as practised before and after 1948. Though denied political freedom, black people could still live and work where they liked, generally speaking, at the time. They could even own property and marry whoever they liked among other blacks. Segregation then did not deny them their humanity and there was hope, generally, that one day whites would change their minds. Then came 1948. Their experience had ever since been a harvest of despair; a total rejection of their very being. The white people seemed all too powerful in their bigoted ways. But black children, as illustrated by the events in Soweto, showed, she said, how through unity and concerted action blacks could regain their manhood and respect; how they could reclaim their dignity and their rights.

Another academic, Herbert Vilakazi, believed separate development contained within itself seeds of self-destruction. Not only was it unable to cope with current economic needs, but the very limited freedom it afforded certain individual groups, coupled with those economic forces, would destroy it. A people would never be satisfied with mere crumbs. The less they got, the more they wanted. Blacks, now being given the right to control only thirteen per cent of the country's land surface, would soon realise it was woefully inadequate and make demands for more. The children of Soweto were a classic example. They were products of Bantu Education and had no other educational experience. Yet they were now rejecting what authorities prescribed because they found it did not fulfill their dreams. There was also historical evidence that apartheid as practised today could not meet the ever growing industrial needs for all forms of labour. Institutional discrimination was, therefore, doomed. It had no future whatsoever.

Blacks were urged to emulate Afrikaners in their struggle for a better life. Afrikaners, author and educationalist Es'kia Mphahlele told the conference, had fully exploited their condition of unfreedom to retain unity among the volk. They upheld that unity by forming exclusive cultural bodies which directed thought and became the guiding spirit of advancement. Such bodies were the bootstraps with which they lifted themselves. Although they had overcome their subjugation and became topdog long ago, their cultural institutions had remained part and parcel of their lives.

Their literature was steeped in and drawn out of their day-to-day experience. There couldn't be a better model for the black people if they were really determined to break down the shackles of bondage.

Looking into the future, the conference pointed out that the Institute of Black Studies could be a good starting point. The organisation could hold similar conferences annually and so sustain continued analysis of the black people's condition. Besides, it could establish branches in various parts of the country and work towards introducing a black studies faculty at each of the existing black universities. It could make it its business, too, conducting intensive research and compiling data, a reservoir from which black scholars could draw materials for writing the black people's history, and sponsoring writers within the black community.

But then these tolerant sentiments, if not the entire conference, represented the old folk, a generation that still only wished for freedom in its lifetime. The wheel had turned round, though, considerably. Black children were alienated, utterly alienated. They no longer had time to argue, to talk. They wanted their freedom right away. They seemed determined to get it by force − if necessary. Property had so far been their target. There would be no official buildings left next time, but they would certainly find other targets.

A few days after the conference closed, Fatima Meer was banned. Then they came for me, hammer and tongs, at noon on Thursday, 29 July.

CHAPTER 6

A NERVOUS WRECK

The swish of the conveyor belt on the ceiling above was barely audible. So was the faint, intermittent rattle from typewriters dotted on messy desks about the newsroom. Only the distant hum of moving traffic outside could be heard. But I did not hear the commissionaire walk up to me.

'Some visitors,' he said.' Can they come in?'

'Ja,' I mumbled, neither looking at him nor paying attention to what he said.

For two weeks I had anxiously been trying to see Tsietsi, the student leader who, like a meteor, had shot up overnight and so shaken the country. Only that morning had I had the good fortune to meet him. Though the meeting had been brief, the lanky, light-skinned but freckle-faced lad had clarified some points and I wanted to put them down while still fresh in my mind before the full-blown interview in the evening. The commissionaire shuffled away. I continued pounding the typewriter.

Then a voice interrupted. I looked up. A stranger, sallow and tall and athletic, with reddish cropped hair on his head, stood beside me. I fidgeted with some papers, covering the top of the machine. He said something. We stared at each other. I expected him to say who he was. He didn't. 'Let's get to the passage,' he said instead. 'I want to talk to you, privately.' He stepped back a little and started moving slowly towards the door as I rose. Who was this man? What did he want from me? The commissionaire must have told him who I was. As he swung the door open it squeaked but he held on to it until I went past.

Two other men (one equally robust and tall but rather older, and one comparatively tiny and youngish-looking) stood in the passage not far from the commissionaire's desk. They came over to us and the man who had led me out of the office then said he was, let's say, Sergeant Rooikop; the others Captain Voor and Steen. They were, he added, security police from John Vorster Square. I was under arrest and would be detained under Section 6 of the Terrorism Act. My heart sank. He also explained that I would not be allowed to talk to anyone but the police.

My children, what would happen to them? Would they continue schooling? There was no one I could think of who could help. What would become of them? Would they really lock me up? For what? I'd done nothing, absolutely nothing. On nothing, so many people had been detained and kept away from their families for months on end. Some had come back, some died there. Still convinced I was as innocent as a dove, I refused to believe they would lock me up. Colleague Graeme Addison emerged into the passage. Looking rather agitated, he hovered around like a hen trying to protect her brood against some impending doom. Haltingly, he asked the men who they were, whether he could help. They were security police, one said, and he warned him not to talk to me. The editor was in charge here, Addison said. Would they talk to him? They would not. He ran down the passage towards the editor's office.

'*Kom* – Come,' Captain Voor said.

'Can I fetch my overcoat?'

They looked at one another.

'*Ja,*' said Sergeant Rooikop. And as we went back into the office I noticed that he was following me.

There was no doubt the newsroom had sensed what was going on. Someone was clearing my desk. He moved hurriedly away and sat at his own desk when he saw us coming. Gesturing, I tried to communicate with him. Another colleague, who seemed thoroughly shaken, held me by the arm. She wished me God's protection as I walked behind the officer. Silent, we stepped down winding stairs, with Voor and Rooikop and Steen close on my heels, out into Sauer Street. The street seemed unusually deserted. We were still climbing into their car, a creamish Volkswagen parked directly in front of the main entrance, with a police sign on the windscreen, when the editor, a piece of a paper in his hand, ran towards us. He stopped in front of the vehicle, then moved to the driver. He wanted to know why I was being detained and, as if in afterthought, asked whether the detention had anything to do with my work as a reporter.

I was stunned. Did the editor think I might have been doing something? Suddenly, I was also thinking of an incident three years back when a black colleague was banned. We were condemning the ban when a female fellow reporter, white, retorted that it should be remembered there couldn't be smoke without fire. Cripes, even the editor did not trust me. He was told by Captain Voor that they did not know, but suggested he telephone Colonel Hoof for any information he might need. He quickly moved out of the way.

We drove off and turned round the corner into Pritchard Street. Captain Voor immediately wanted to know what the book I was writing was all about. The book! Someone must have told them about it. So this was my crime. Not surprising, really. Quite a lot of people already knew of the book project I was working on. We had been researching material for it for almost a month now. Some bereaved families, whose children died during the upheavals had told me that BOSS (Bureau of State Security) warned them not to talk to anyone about their children's deaths. Besides virtually everybody in the newsroom knew. So did many, many others, most of them students I had interviewed. So it was not surprising, especially in a country riddled through and through with police informers, that BOSS had been tipped off. 'It's about students' unrest from 1972 right up to the rioting last June,' I said.

'Where will it be published?'

'No arrangements have been made.'

I was being detained, he said, because they wanted information from me on everything I knew about the riots and meetings held in Soweto since 16 June. Believing I had done nothing criminal, I slowly calmed down as we cruised down Pritchard Street and turned left into Diagonal Street, crossed President and Market streets, then right into West Street and immediately swung right into Commissioner Street towards John Vorster Square down the road.

At the Soweto meetings, a mass burial of the hundreds who died from police shootings and beatings on that fateful Wednesday and subsequent days had been planned. The BPA, which had planned and held the meetings, did not defy the Minister of Justice after he banned the mass burial. Instead, it had compromised by holding one symbolic funeral service for Hector Pieterson. By focusing attention on one burial service, no matter how massive and symbolic, the leaders had avoided a bloody confrontation (between police and students) which, I reckoned, even police should have appreciated. These people had merely involved themselves in burying the dead and it was not yet a crime for Africans in South Africa to bury their dead. Besides, all the meetings and the symbolic funeral had been extensively reported in the press. There was, therefore, nothing to hide.

But something still troubled my conscience. Would it be right to give names of either the people who arranged these meetings or those who had given me interviews? Hadn't they invited me to the meetings or opened their hearts to me because they trusted me? Would I not be breaking that trust, betraying them, if I yielded? Another equally agonising question reared its head. If I refused to talk, would the police not conclude these meetings or people were involved in some plot? The Volkswagen sped past John Vorster, heading towards Soweto.

Once more fear struck. They were going to search my home! Typed notes and letters related to the book project were all there. They would confiscate them, I thought. The many other documents stored in the office in town, would they be safe? Was I stupid in first place to embark on this sort of thing? Detention, just like death, is so common here. We talk glibly about it daily, yet we panic when it comes our way. The trouble was that one never knew whether he would come back or not. Many came back, many died there. That's the trouble. I was a political prisoner now, but for what? No idea. The thought petrified me.

We entered the vast labour camp called Soweto through the New Canada motorway. Young children, here and there, wallowed in the dusty streets that criss-crossed the settlement; charred vehicles, symbols of the rioting that erupted after the shootings, still littered the roadsides. A riot car, two men in the driver's cabin, pulled out of Orlando Police Station, heading in the opposite direction; two elderly fruit and vegetable vendors sat forlornly near their wares at the nearby bus stop, west of the station. With its symmetrical matchbox cottages and without the usual crowds in the streets, Soweto looked ghostlier than ever. I was physically locked up in the vehicle, but mentally I was far away, at home in Naledi, turning things upside down to see what stuff lay there in the notebooks, files, the book shelf.

The tiny vehicle swung left as we approached the Orlando overhead railway bridge, into the road to Nancefield, then to Klipspruit and right into the road to old Potchesfstroom Road, heading towards Moroka Police Station beyond the now gutted Chinese business section. We were not going to my home, after all. Otherwise, they would be asking for the way, I thought. The thought comforted me a bit. They knew where we were going, but I dared not ask. Barely forty minutes after leaving the office, we arrived at Protea, divisional Police headquarters for Soweto.

Protea, a cluster of blocks of red brick-walled buildings situated in a hollow among tall trees on a farm just behind the Soweto complex, was once a Roman Catholic home for orphaned coloured girls. The Good Shepherd, it was called then. And there, the inmates chanted the rosary while being taught that love and respect for life were the highest values before God. But Good Shepherd was no more. The farm had been taken over by the government under the Group Areas Act and declared an African area. Good Shepherd had to go. So did its spiritual function. Protea had since assumed a new character. We entered one of the blocks of the buildings through a side door into a passage and immediately turned left, walking along the passage. A steel barricade, locked. Captain Voor pressed a button on the barricade. We waited.

Then a muscular, towering, dark-haired fellow − wearing a navy-blue blazer, blue shirt, tie and dark glasses − strode towards us. He opened the barricade, we stepped in. He said something to the other police as we walked along, passing a door on the left. Outside the next door, also on the left, we waited while the police continued talking in whispers a little away from me. After about five minutes another man arrived. The burly man (I later got to know his name, Captain Heystek) opened the barricade steel gate for him. He joined us. It's unforgettable, the face of grey-haired, hefty but slightly stooped Major Skalkwyk Visser, head of the security police at Protea. Was this Colonel Hoof? I wondered.

'We found him,' Sergeant Rooikop said, talking to Visser.

'Have you told him everything?' Visser enquired.

'No, we only told him that we want information from him on his book and the riots.'

'Where are pamphlets?' Visser snarled, staring me in the eye.

'What pamphlets, sir?' I said.

'You know we kill terrorists on the border, but we do worse things to people like you. Where are the pamphlets?' he barked again.

I grinned sheepishly.

He spun round and fidgeted with the door, asking me to come in. I followed. Heystek walked closely behind me. Visser hurried to his desk, pulled off his grey jacket, hung it over the chair behind the desk and came to meet me in the middle of the room.

'Where are the pamphlets?' Visser barked yet again.

'What pamphlets, sir? I don't…'

He slapped me on the side of the face and, as my spectacles flew off, followed with a stiff punch to the chest. As I staggered back, Heystek, standing on the side, chopped me with a solid karate punch on the back of my neck. I folded up instantly. When I eventually came round (I don't know after how long), strangely enough I was thinking about Joseph Mdluli (he died on 19 March 1976 soon after his detention). My head was racked with pain; water had been poured over me, my pockets emptied (I could see all my articles or things lying on the desk). This is how Mdluli died, I was thinking.

'This one will die,' Heystek was saying, disturbing my whirling thoughts. 'He's too weak, he mustn't die before telling us about the pamphlets.'

Visser, silent and staring at the floor, strode menacingly up and down the room like a wild animal.

'Get up,' Heystek snarled when he noticed I was battling to rise. I summoned all my power, but still could not get up. He helped me to a chair. I complained of an acute, splitting headache. He produced out of his pocket some tablets, trying to give them to me. I refused and suggested to him to give me the Codice tablets now lying within the bundle on the desk which I happened to have had on me. He repeatedly wanted to know where the pamphlets were; I repeatedly wanted to know what pamphlets, beseechingly saying I did not know what pamphlets he wanted from me. Did I want to be a martyr, he laughed, rather than tell them about the pamphlets? I was completely at a loss.

'Where do you live, 835 Dube?' Visser, still stern, asked.

'586A Naledi.'

'Don't you live at 835 Dube?'

'I once did, before I was given the house in Naledi.'

Travelling in two cars, the police took me to my home. Children scattered from Mahune Street, fleeing into the yards on the sides as we approached, a cloud of dust behind us. They stood watching from their yards. I unlocked the gate, led Visser and Hystek in. We entered through the back door into the kitchen. Visser led the way into the living room and then peered into the children's bedroom. 'It's the wrong place,' he moaned. 'Are you sure you live here?' he stared at me. He moved to the main bedroom, opened the door, entered and cried out, 'We will sure find what we want. Ask Voor to come in.' Heystek went out and returned with Voor.

For almost two hours I watched helplessly as my bedroom and bookshelf were turned upside down, the entire room littered with books and newspaper clippings. There still were no pamphlets, but the police removed notebooks, typed scripts, two personal files, numerous books, newspaper cutting and my typewriter. The notebooks and typed scripts were poured into my two briefcases. Then we moved out. At about 5pm or soon thereafter we reached John Vorster Square, which was to be my home for the next four months.

We entered the massive concrete building through the garage at the back. An automatic lift, situated at the far western corner, zoomed us, without stopping anywhere along the way, right up to the notorious Tenth Floor. (It was from here that Ahmed Timol 'jumped' through a window to his death on the ground below while under police interrogation in October 1971). Visser, carrying the two briefcases, led the way. We turned right, walking along a very long passage. There were offices on either side of the passage. Some of the offices were closed, some were open and I could clearly see Johannesburg South and some mine dumps in the distance. The streets were jammed with traffic, the end of day traffic. Suddenly, I was thrown into a room towards the end of the passage. And the room was crammed with men. Like vultures to a carcass, they descended on me.

'So this is the reporter, the Communist writer,' cried a voice from within the room.

'Get this straight,' said another. 'We'll not take any of your Communist shit. We want the truth, nothing but facts, hear?'

Never before had I felt so lonely, so helpless.

Where were the pamphlets; did I belong to any political movement, know Abram Fischer, Helen Joseph; what was Black Consciousness; did I know Winnie Mandela, Joe Slovo, Margaret Smith, Sheila Weinberg? The questions came fast and in quick succession. They were hurled at me from all over the room. And they were mingled with solid *klaps*, kicks and shouts of 'can't you stand properly, bloody Communist.' Never before had I come across such an over-zealous mob. They were not even interested in answers to the very questions they asked! I was baffled to no end. Fearing they might break my eyeglasses, I had taken them off and placed them on the table in the middle of the room when they first pounced. They did not force me to put them on.

'Why don't you give me a chance to answer your questions, officer?' I cried out, not referring to anyone in particular.

'Who's officer,' a man slapped me, 'don't officer me bastard.'

'See, he writes good stories about Winnie Mandela, but calls us pigs,' someone said, obviously reading the notes confiscated from my home, and sounded very angry. Moved and beaten, I felt weary and in deep despair. And it was not until about midnight that the viciousness slightly abated. Most interrogators had quietly melted away. But behind me still stood the only African, who had so far been there but uninvolved in the torture. Occasionally he had hurled abuse, but no more. Red-eyed, apparently from lack of sleep, he was stern and seemed equally devoid of human feeling. But there was a false ring in his voice whenever he barked. All along, his job had seemed to have been to attend to the needs of my tormentors. He had made tea or brought them water whenever these things were needed.

The gaunt white officer, perched on the table before me with his legs dangling, still awed me. While striking me with a ruler (I wondered where he got it) on the neck, he warned he would give me three minutes to tell him the truth. Otherwise, he would kill me. He said he knew everything, but wanted me to say it voluntarily. And he hoped, he said, I understood what he meant. I felt utterly helpless, but cried, rather like an automaton, that I understood him. A movement outside. Apparently from another room along the passage. But I was too weary, beat up and drained to pay any particular attention. The door opened and someone said: 'How you faring?' The officer in front of me shook his head. 'It looks like our man is letting us down,' he said. The short officer, who had just entered the room, then said: 'My man is already writing his statement.' Then he went out, closing the door behind him, to whoever he was interrogating.

'I want facts, the truth. Not the nonsense you write in the newspaper, understand?' said the gaunt officer next to me. He added, 'Do you know anybody in Cape Town?'

'Yes, Anthony Richmond; he once worked with me.'

'Think properly if there's no one else you know.'

'Absolutely no one,' I said.

'Did you read newspaper this morning?'

'No, I didn't.

'Why?'

'I was working in Soweto and did not have time to read anything.'

'Who is that? He shoved a copy of *The Rand Daily Mail* at me, pointing a picture on the front page. I picked up my glasses from the table and, using them, looked at the picture.

'It's Tony Holiday, he looks older here.'

'No, he's not old; what do you know about him?'

'He's a political reporter for *The Rand Daily Mail*.'

Don't lie to me.' he barked. 'You know he works for the *Cape Times*.'

'I don't know that.'

'When last did you see him?'

'About six years ago.'

'Don't lie, we know everything. Holiday has confessed that he has been working with you printing and distributing ANC pamphlets,' he said.

I was stunned. 'It's a lie.' My mind whirled and whirled. So this was it. Besides the book, I was supposed to be involved in some plot. It had so far been relatively easy to answer queries related to the book project. But how did one explain his position over an issue he knew nothing about, especially in the midst of so much hostility, hate and terror? 'It's a lie,' I repeated again. He stared into my eyes. Nothing could be more heart-rending. How could I convince this man? Once again, I cried plaintively, 'It's a lie, Holiday was lying.' But the more I said that Holiday had lied to them, the more he hit me. Truth was a mere ploy in his mind. It might have been better, I felt, if I had in fact been involved, for then I would at least be suffering for what I had actually done and not as a result of an outrageous lie. The officer pursued his line to link me, no matter my protestations, with other people. Holiday must have named him too as a co-conspirator.

'Do you know Patrick Weech?' he wanted to know.

'No, I don't know him.'

'He was working with you, you should know him.'

'Does he say he knows me?'

'I'm asking you questions, don't ask me.'

'I am sorry officer. It's just that I don't know him.'

Believing the self-confessed ANC operative had told the truth and that I was lying, the security officer ordered me to half-squat, with arms raised and open hands touching above the head (detainees call it sitting on an imaginary chair). In that position, I soon discovered, the weight of my body rested on the knees. Within barely fifteen minutes the whole body sweated. A trickle of sweat flowed from armpits on either sides of the body, which felt as if it had been immersed in steam. Though somewhat taut, the body also quivered. Boom, I collapsed on my back on the concrete floor. He kicked and shouted at me to get up. So did the African. I stretched my legs a little as I got up, getting back into position. From about 3am until 8am, I half-squatted, collapsed, was kicked, stretched legs, got into position only to fall down again and again and again. The agony was killing and, some moments, I even regretted ever having regained consciousness in Visser's office at Protea. I reckoned then I would have died peacefully for the karate blow and its effect had been instantaneous. Except for a strange sensation during which I did not feel suspended, but simply floated in space. Everything became painlessly still all at once.

For more than twelve hours I had been standing. I had had nothing to eat, but I felt no hunger. Only my body ached, terribly. All illusions that they would not kill me had evaporated; thought of the outside world, including my own family, had vanished. 'Sleep on the chair,' said the security policeman. It was an armchair. I could not sleep.

Overnight, I had become a nervous wreck. My right eye and my mouth were bruised and my neck was stiff. Also, I breathed with difficulty, with an excruciating pain in my chest. My left arm was lamer than when I woke up after the attack at Protea. Each time I caught some sleep, I would wake up with a start almost immediately. More and more interrogators were returning. I could hear movements in the passage and doors opening and closing. Another day had begun.

CHAPTER 7

IN THE ABYSS

The night in the abyss had been revealing in many ways. June 16 caught the police and their informers with their pants down. They believed, wrongly, that Communists, through the BPA, had organised the uprising. And they wanted to use us to prove their unfounded notions.

Soon after eight-thirty, I was led out of the interrogation room. Handcuffed, I was led through the eastern end of the passage on the Tenth floor, past a steel barricade, down winding stairs on the ninth floor below. From there, we took a lift out of the building. With the armed escort, we then walked across to the charge office on the eastern wing of John Vorster Square.

The charge office was crammed with uniformed police, white and black, and other souls who seemed just as beat up as I was. Here I was stripped of two ballpoint pens, my belt and a nail clipper. All of them articles that, they said, I could use to commit suicide. Also, the few coins I had were taken way. The articles and the money were given to a white policeman for storage. I was duly handed a receipt. There was no one I knew among the equally miserable people in the charge office. Then we wound our way towards the interior. An African constable opened a steel door. We walked past and through yet another steel door to a lift. It carried us up the building and came to a halt on the second floor. Out we went and entered, through yet another steel door. The door was closed behind us. Then we walked along a particularly clean passage, with particularly dirty walls on either side. There were cells on either side of the passage. We shuffled along and suddenly stopped outside cell number 218, my new home. The escort produced a bundle of keys with which he opened the door. An inner door, made of steel bars and also locked, stood in the rear. He opened that too. 'You'll stay in here,' he said. I stepped in and, standing a little away from the door, looked back at him as he locked me in.

My new home, with high dusty grey walls, was self-contained. It had a toilet with running water, three built-in concrete bunks alongside the inner wall and against the two side walls. Sunlight filtered in through two rear windows, with steel security mesh wire. There was also another barricaded window on the side of the doors in front. An electric light was embedded on the high plain concrete ceiling above. The ceiling was so high up that one could reach it only with a ladder. A sullied mattress, with equally filthy blankets on top, was abandoned at the corner alongside the southern wall. The mattress and blankets seemed a nest for bugs, lice. But I was too tired and drained to worry about such pests really. I moved over to sit on the bunk along the far wall next to a plate and a mug with a spoon inside. I could hear the policeman's footsteps fade away. The mattress and blankets were so filthy it seemed they had been put there just to mock whatever gentility I might have claimed. A screeching, banging sound echoed through the cell complex as the steel door at the entrance opened and closed; then again as the lift squeaked open and closed. Almost immediately, someone coughed in the cell opposite and another further away. There were, I thought, other people around. And the thought was comforting.

'Hi, brother,' a voice said.' Get to the window so we can talk.'

I listened. Silence.

'I'm talking to you, you just arrived,' the voice continued.

Who could this be? I wondered. Why did he want to talk to me? Did he want to get into more trouble? Fearful, distrustful, I remained quiet, pretending not to hear in spite of the fact that his presence somehow made so much difference. He stopped calling. I took off my shoes and jacket, placed them on the bunk nearer the mattress and dug in, trousers and all, under the dirty blankets. With a start, I woke up. The outer door swung open, banging against the wall. A uniformed African policeman stared me in the face through the inner steel barricade. '*Ukudla,*' he said and moved away to the opposite cell. A chap carrying a bucket and furtively glancing this way and that shuffled toward the door. He asked for the mug.

I hurried to the bunk, grabbed it out of the plate and handed it over to him through the locked steel barricade. Another chappie, carrying a large carton, joined him. Winking, they gave me coffee and two large slices of brown bread. And as they moved to the opposite cell where the inmate already stood waiting, three others carrying steel pots, came over and stood at the door. One of them asked me for the plate and, as I handed it over, whispered to me, 'I'm also a "Black Power", from Klipspruit; where do you come from?' His head was dotted with scars. A thug, I thought. He dropped a couple of spoonfuls of maize samp, mincemeat and cabbage onto the plate before giving it back. Then he moved away. He was also a black power; what did he mean? I wondered. Perhaps that was his way of saying he was also a detainee or was he just trying to show his sympathy? I could not believe he was a detainee, but the possibility persisted.

The policeman turned. He locked the outer door after enquiring whether I received all the lunch rations. As he went away, I went to sit on the bunk diagonally opposite the door and began eating. The stamp mealies were well cooked and nice, the mince saltless and the cabbage overcooked, tasteless. The coffee was cold and too sweet. And what made it even harder to drink was the fact that the sandwiches were smothered with jam. After the meal I stood watching outside through one of the frosted rear windows that was open.

A big courtyard divided the cells on the row from others on another along the eastern outer block. The yard seemed far below the second floor. It must be level with the ground floor. I thought. Also visible was a portion of the third floor, its north-eastern wing, and a tiny portion of the sky. Totally obscured were the views to the south, the west and the north.

The outer door, with its characteristic peephole, was eloquent. So were the walls. 'Help the Coons – vote Nat' said one of the legends scrawled on the walls. Another, on the back of the outer door, simply mocked: 'Crime don't Pay and You're Well-comed at John Vorster's Criminal Club.' One of the former inmates had even drawn a portrait of a white woman, possibly his lover. But each time I looked at the drawing, I felt she must have jilted him before he came into the abyss; and he must have been bitter about it to portray her so horribly. A list of notorious township gangs and thugs that had, at one time or another, terrorised Johannesburg – Msomi Gang, Spoilers, Khorombi and Boy Faraday, among them – was also pencilled faintly on the short wall which partially partitioned the toilet. Slowly but surely, boredom crept in. The legends had cheered me a bit, but there was nothing else. The thought that I might be kept here for weeks, if not months, simply killed, over-powered me.

After dinner (it was no different from the lunch), the man in the opposite cell once again called on me to get to the window so that we could talk. Hesitantly, I complied. He was young, and bushy-haired. T-O, he said, was his name. Quickly, he explained that detainees used codes, not real names, to avoid detection for they were not allowed to talk to one another. They also stood closer to open windows when talking to deflect voices because, he said, the cells were bugged. You had to speak with your mouth against the security mesh covering the windows and talk while facing out into the passage. That way, T-O said, you cheated the bugging device.

T-O was also a Section 6 detainee. He came from Tladi and, like me, had been picked up from his place of employment in the city. It was his second week in the abyss. He had always stayed alone in the cell. His mother had visited Pietersburg in the northern

Transvaal, leaving him with her younger children, his brothers and sisters. He did not know how they were coping without him. That worried him in no small way. There was also no one to bring him clean clothes. 'Don't worry, everything will be okay,' I said without much conviction in the veracity of what I said.

There was a terrible pain in my chest. Each time I coughed I felt as if my ribs were broken, with the broken bits piercing the insides, and my left arm was lame. I told T–O too how I came to be in that condition.

A school drop-out, T–O said he had dropped out of school because of poverty. He was working in order to help his mother, a factory worker herself, educate the younger children. He was the eldest child in the family and didn't want his brothers and sisters to be faced with the same prospect of having to drop out of school. His wish for them was university education. Then he wanted to know who the white man in the third cell along the same row was. He was, he explained, brought in that morning too, but a little earlier. I had not seen him, I said.

Someone whistled.

I took fright. The whistling echoed within the prison cells.

'*Eskies.*' T–O grated, running to the back of his cell and, as soon as the echo died down, opened one of the windows. Then he whistled too.

'T–O (it sounded to me like Teo). T–R on the line,' an echo bounced, then died down

'*Ja,* T–O listening.'

'Come again?'

'T–O on the line. L–i–s–t–e–n–i–n–g.'

In a gibberish, they began shouting at each other and laughing. I couldn't follow what they said, but I was intrigued. At the end of their talk, T–O said T–R wanted to know whether there had been any new arrivals. He had told him of me and the white man down the passage. T-R, said T-O, was a student leader from Soweto. He had already spent about four weeks in detention (could it be Seth, I wondered). They had a friend, T-Z. He occupied a cell at the extreme end of the second floor, overlooking Market Street. He explained too that I would be given my detention name the next day. Speaking of more other detainees living there, T-O said some had been there for almost a year, without any charges being laid against them, and some had been detained soon after the outbreak of the upheavals. Two came from Durban in Natal and the rest from Soweto and Alexandra townships in Johannesburg. Most of the cells across the court-yard behind me housed woman detainees, he said.

Somewhere within the hollow edifice someone began singing. His voice, uninspiring, floated through the cells. It sounded as if he was trying to sing a hymn, but was simply pining, not singing.

'Who could that be?' I asked

'T-R, I think. He likes singing,' T-O said.

'Are you allowed to sing?'

'No,' he laughed. 'We just sing when it's safe to while away time.'

'Is it safe now?'

'*Ja,* the doctors and nurses have gone home.'

'Doctors and nurses, what do you mean?'

'We call white interrogators doctors and the black policemen nurses.'

How on earth security police could be likened to doctors and nurses was beyond my comprehension, but I let it go.

'Don't they work at night?'

'They do. Usually on the Tenth floor. They can't hear us from there.'

'But you said the cells are bugged, didn't you?

'Even if they hear they'll not know from which cell the noise comes because it buzzes all over the place.'

T-O was convinced their voices couldn't be heard from outside the cells. But from within, he said, they could hear police when they came in. They heard them when they entered the lift on the ground floor; also when they got out of the lift on the second floor and when they opened or closed it. By the time they reached the second floor all would be quiet.

I excused myself and retreated from the window to sit on the dirty mattress at the corner. Everything chilled. I wanted to find out his real name and those of his friends, but feared he might think I was a plant. Fear, intermingled with suspicion and distrust, weighed heavily on my mind. That was the new life. The future seemed completely shattered. Maybe if I were young, I could also be taking things lightly. Or was I just being cowardly, too intimidated, to feel the way I did? It was an extremely agonising new condition to accept.

The next morning I told Sergeant Chiskop, an African who had been sent to see to it that we showered, that I was ill. I could not breathe because of pain in the chest. Nor could I turn my neck sideways. He would, he said, tell Sergeant Toti, a white policeman. Later that Saturday morning, he returned to say that Toti would take me to the district surgeon on Monday.

We were not allowed to talk to one another even in the shower rooms, although we washed side by side.

Toti, an old man apparently entrusted with the task of seeing to it that our bruised, twisted and torn bodies were mended, was accompanied by Sergeant Ahmed, an Indian youngster. They were both armed and Ahmed made a great show of his revolver. Two other detainees, aged eighteen years, were in the group. We were to be taken to the district surgeon. I did not know them and was never able to find out who they were. They had been beaten. The two cops took us, handcuffed, to the Tenth Floor. Half a carton, filled with bloodied sand, was tucked away in a corner at the entrance outside the passage on the Tenth Floor.

Someone had spat or vomited blood into the carton, I thought. I suspected it must have been a detainee. (I was to see the carton there for several months, each time with its horrifying contents).

We stepped into the passage and stood outside an office. Toti went in and collected some papers. Then we went down the passage, and took the automatic lift into the garage. The handcuffs were removed after we got into the car. We drove into town. I saw no one I knew in the streets. We reached the Department of Health in Harrison Street. The district surgeon attended to us individually but, surprisingly, in the presence of the police. Why did the doctor see us in front of police? Didn't he know they did not want us to talk of our experiences? Whatever his attitude or what might follow, I quickly made up my mind to reveal all. Not only to enable him to make an accurate diagnosis, but also bring to his notice the brutal treatment I got.

Toti was annoyed by my revelations to the district surgeon. But, surprisingly, our doctor was not surprised. He prescribed pain-killers and suggested I must be taken elsewhere for X-rays on the chest and neck. We returned to base. Toti did not have time, he said, to take me in for the X-rays. He was too busy! In vain I waited for him the next morning. He did not turn up until about 2pm. Again in the company of Ahmed. They took me to Bargwanath Hospital. But the queue at the casualty department was too long. Toti tried to facilitate matters by first seeing the hospital superintendent. However, I still had to join the long queue. Nobody took notice of Toti and Ahmed. They might have been important at John Vorster, but at the hospital they were nobodies.

'Let's go. This queue is too long. What do you think?' Toti said, in a surprisingly friendly manner, after having lingered there for more than half an hour. 'Seeing we are already here,' I ventured, 'we may just as well wait and get done with it.'

He did not seem to be listening. He was staring at the chief clerk, the black man who had told him I had to join the queue, police or not. Then he spun round. 'Let's go.' His tone had changed. He walked away, rather in a huff, with Ahmed and I following behind, to the car.

'I'll never send any case to this place,' Toti said as he drove out. 'It's terrible.'

'When we write about the bad treatment people get at this hospital you accuse us of Communism,' I mumbled, somewhat nervously.

'You can write as much as you want. It's bad,' he said. We laughed.

By Friday afternoon, Toti had taken me to four more doctors – two radiologists, a nerve surgeon and an orthopaedic surgeon. A neck brace was prescribed, with orders that I should wear it for at least two months. My chest was not crushed as I had feared. It had become excruciatingly sore because the neck and shoulders, said the doctors, had been damaged. That also was the reason for the lameness of the left arm. A bone at the base of the neck had shifted out of position. 'You're lucky to be still alive; it's a miracle,' the doctors had said. Because the police did not want the world to know they had brutalised me, members of my family were not allowed to see me. They could only send me fruit and cigarettes or bring clean clothing once fortnightly. But other detainees were allowed visits by relations. I reckoned I would only be allowed visits after the neck brace had been removed, possibly at the end of September or beginning of October.

On 19 August, I laid a charge of assault against Captain Heystek and Major Visser. The charge was laid before two senior officers at John Voster Square, but the two men were not keen to take it up. 'You're given good treatment. The assault is not serious,' said one of the officers. 'I think,' I said, 'I'm the only person who can say how serious or not serious the assault is.'

'What do you mean?'

'I want to lay a charge, that's what I mean.'

The officers looked at each other.

'Okay,' said one. Then they referred me to another office, where I made a statement.

That week T–O disappeared from the abyss. He was released, I thought. And the thought accentuated the loneliness and despair of solitary confinement, despite the occasional illicit nocturnal singing. A couple of days after the disappearance of T–O (I think it was on a Saturday or Sunday evening), there was commotion somewhere in the neighborhood. Someone was being beaten in a cell. Crying and pleading for mercy, he was repeatedly bashed against the walls. One could hear his tormentors pounding him. For two days he cried. Shrill at first, his cry became faint as time dragged on. Murder, what was it if not the calculated crushing of a man's body against concrete walls until he died from bleeding through the nose, ears and mouth or internally? I pondered endlessly, unable to sleep. I wished the kid, whoever he was, would have the courage to tell the magistrates, who periodically (once fortnightly to be exact) visited us, about the brutal attacks. But then I remembered the visits were as useless as a dodo. A mere formality. Nothing more. When once I asked one of the magistrate to whom we had repeatedly reported our grievances and requests why these complaints and requests were not attended to, he explained there was nothing they could do, other than pass complaints to senior security officers, hoping they would restrain the juniors dealing directly with us! It was a painful revelation. Even official magistrates, the very custodians of the law, could not help detainees! Detainees were entirely at the mercy of the ruthless interrogators, as family lawyers also had no access to them.

Ebullient Mokoena, who together with Tsietsi and others had been on the run since early July, arrived in the abyss one morning towards the end of August or early September. He was confined to a cell diagonally opposite 218. We spotted each other at breakfast time while standing behind the barricaded doors, waiting for rations. He was not wearing his spectacles. He made the black power salute greeting. I wondered what he thought of the brace round my neck. His spectacles were broken when he was assaulted after his arrest, he later explained. Other new arrivals, also along the row, were four matric students from four Soweto schools – Morris Isaacson, Orlando West High, Naledi and Sekano-Ntoane. They had all been picked up from their homes.

The boy from Naledi occupied T-O's cell and Mokoena was on his left. On his right, they had thrown in the youngster from Morris Isaacson, while the boy from Orlando West was in the cell on my left. On my right the chappie from Sekano-Ntoane. Through Mokoena, whom I knew very well, I got to know the school boys. Their presence had a warm, enlivening effect. We communicated with ease. Either through the mail, delivered at meal times, or through howling at one another whenever possible. We could write because, unlike me, they had not been stripped of ballpoint pens and I had got one as a gift. I also discovered that Tizza, the BPC secretary-general, had been staying along the row weeks before my arrival.

The kid from Morris Isaacson, confident and brash, was an outright exhibitionist. He would talk endlessly, not only about what he was going to do after his release, but also about the good time he had had with girls, his girlfriends. He didn't care, he often said, about his education any more. There were far important things to do in the liberation struggle. The Sekano-Ntoane chappie was just as garrulous, though less articulate and intelligent. He considered himself an outcast in his family and was involved in student politics despite his parent's bitter opposition. He was bitter, possibly on account of the poor family relationship, and sounded rather keen to see the struggle going on. His other obsession was music. He had once received lessons from a private music tutor in the suburbs in Johannesburg. He wanted to continue studying music, possibly in America. In contrast, the boy from Orlando West and the one from Naledi were relatively subdued, but sounded more honest and convincing. They also seemed far more concerned about their academic studies. The Orlando West kid, who had a heart condition, was, however, more positive about his academic future, while the fellow from Naledi seemed to have not quite made up his mind. He seemed torn between going to university to do law and helping his father run the family store at Westonaria.

But whatever their personalities, the schoolboys were good company. And we shared the food parcels, which sometimes dropped in from home. It was Mokoena, however, who was and remained the soul of the group. I had not known he was such a fine singer, nor that he was such a deeply religious man. In addition, the chaps who served us at mealtimes were our heroes. They were not detainees though. They were awaiting-trial prisoners, and had been arrested for various offences – stealing, robbery, loitering and pick-pocketing. But they were treated far better than detainees. And, in fact, they were so free that some even sold dagga in the cells. Without them, we detainees would have been doomed, for confidential communication lines could never have opened.

Tizza had just completed a two-week long uninterrupted interrogation. He had stood day in, day out, eating his food rations in that position, for two weeks running, while three interrogators took turns questioning him. The only time he had some kind of rest was when he visited the toilet. And they always made sure he didn't go to the loo simply to cheat. He was brought into his cell at the end of the two weeks. I noticed that he could no longer walk; he hobbled. His legs were so swollen he seemed to be suffering from elephantisis.

The honeymoon ended. More and more new detainees were coming in, virtually every day. They were even placed in cells on the third floor and, in some cases, police put two to three detainees in a cell. Food rations became scantier than before. As always, we complained to the visiting magistrates, requesting more grub. But it all came to naught.

'You haven't come here to be fattened,' the kid from Morris Isaacson was rudely reminded when he complained to one of the African security men. Daily interrogations were stepped up too, with detainees beaten to endorse lies and so incriminate themselves or others. They reeled backwards and forwards in the corridors and interrogation rooms. A burly security officer who was interrogating the kid from Naledi High ordered him to lie down during a lunch break. Then, the kid told us that night, he sat on top of him and had his lunch. Cripes!

Once again, Soweto was on the boil. A student march through the heart of Johannesburg had been frustrated by the police on 4 August. Students had since been compelling parents to stay away from work in protest against continuous detentions and fatal shootings. Police had sown discord among the people, in a bid to break down their solidarity. Hostel-dwellers at Mzimhlope Hostel were fighting with township residents. They directed their venom, stirred up anger, at students. That was why the population in the abyss increased, why interrogations were stepped up.

Captain Cronwright. He was tiny, with a Hitlerian moustache, hawk-like eyes and slender shoulders. He wore a grey suit and almost always had a gun on his hip beneath his jacket. Though thinnish in stature, he had felled many a victim in the course of his duty, while extracting 'statements'. He was the kind of man in whose presence even his fellow policemen fretted, trying to humour him. So when he summoned me to his office on the Tenth Floor on 10 September, I felt rotten inside.

Another interrogation spell? He stood alone in the middle of his office, pensively looking down. I waited, watching him, as the African security escort faintly knocked at the open door. He looked up, his face contorted.

'I'll not take any of your shit,' he rattled. 'You wear that collar pretending to be sick. It's costing us a lot of money each day you're supposed to be wearing it. I want you to take it off, you hear?'

I nodded.

'Take him to the cells and come back with that collar,' Captain Cronwright ordered the escort.

We stepped out.

I could not eat, sleep nor talk to anyone that day. What was all this? What did it portend? I felt helpless.

Three days later my wife arrived! She had at long last got permission to see me. We met in an executive, carpeted office on the ninth floor. The visit was meaningless, for I could not tell her anything in the presence of a policeman. Later, a neighbour in the abyss suggested that when she next visited I should go to meet her with a note crumbled in my mouth so that when I kissed her I could drop it in her mouth. What if she spat it on the floor, because she would not be expecting any such thing? It was too risky. I would be in hell thereafter. We laughed off the suggestion. Anyway, I consoled myself that those detainees who might be released before me would be man enough to tell the family or my employers about my condition.

There was commotion in the courtyard behind 218 at about 4pm one day. I wondered what was going on as I sat there on the bunk reading the Bible, the only book I was allowed. Eventually, I went to the window to check. The courtyard was crammed with men, most of them young. The Orlando West school boy was already talking to some of them. A kid was telling him they had been arrested in the city while marching through the streets.

Soweto students had penetrated the city in a protest march! How did they do it? Did police simply overlook them marching from the townships into the city? Incredible. '*Leriri, ke leriri* – army, it's an army,' someone shouted from his cell. 'We shall overcome,' he said.

But some nut on the third floor began hurling abuse at the crowd in the courtyard. '*Kaffirs*, you bastards. All you can do is fuck your own mothers,' he said. But a group within the crowd hit back: 'Bloody boer, white scum; that's what you are.'

A white hobo, I thought.

Incessantly, they hurled abuse at each other.

'Quiet,' shouted a white security cop as he and two others entered the courtyard. Silence fell over the courtyard. The officer sorted out the crowd. The people shuffled this way and that. Students were separated and grouped according to their schools. Workers were also ordered to stand on one side. So were those who were neither scholars nor workers. Then the workers and the unemployed were led in separate groups out of the courtyard.

As soon as the two officers went out, the 'white scum' on the third floor poured water on the students. He used a hose. The scholars, whistling, scampered all over the yard. But it was not until sunset that the scantily-clothed kids were removed from the place. However, they were brought back later. Each had been given a blanket. Later that evening, we learnt from the grapevine that the children had surprised a sedate Johannesburg. They had sneaked into the city and attacked shops as they marched down the street. Hundreds had been arrested. They spent the night right there in the open courtyard.

'*Ke leriri,*' said a neighbour after we'd heard what happened. We were taking comfort from the pressure they exerted on the system. The food situation improved after some time. Some victims had gone. In our row the Morris Isaacson kid was the first to go. He went home. So did the Orlando West boy, we thought. But he returned hardly three weeks later. He had been transferred, apparently because of his heart condition, to Norwood where, we understood, conditions were far better than at John Vorster. He was brought back after a colleague had, unsuccessfully, attempted to escape.

Mathabathe, the Morris Isaacson High School principal, had been with us in the abyss for some time. But Soweto was rife with rumour that he was dead. He and Mokoena were going through a difficult period. Statements extracted from them were repeatedly rejected. They were subjected to an eighteen-hour uninterrupted interrogation. It began at eight each morning and ended at about

2am the next day. That meant they had lunches and dinners standing up. After the first week, they were subjected to another week of twenty-four-hour continuous interrogation.

Kneeling on the concrete floor during prolonged interrogation broke Mokoena. In desperation, he claimed responsibility for events he knew nothing about. How else could he have said that he incited school children to riot on 16 June? Kneeling (he called it kneeology) was the severest from of torture, he said. He had never been subjected to anything like that before. On the other hand, Mathabathe had stuck to his guns. He refused to swallow the lies that he had been working in cahoots with his students or that his school was a Communist cell.

'They would rather kill me,' he said. And we feared they would. It was indeed a very rough time. The Naledi school boy started behaving in a manner that made us feel he was going bananas. Though we were used to him wondering aloud when he would be released, we panicked when he began sending private messages to individuals asking, 'When do you think I shall be released?' or, 'Will we ever go home?' And as if that was not enough, he borrowed my Bible, the only one available along the row. Not to read it, but to rest his head on it when sleeping at night! Otherwise, he said he was unable to sleep. The boy, we feared, was losing his senses. But what could we do to help him? He became more subdued and, occasionally, told us he was going to be charged. He knew, he said, because he had had a dream. Thus we were relieved when he was eventually whisked away in October. We thought he had gone home. But he had been taken to Langlaagte Police cells for isolation.

One morning while I was admiring sunbeams filtering through the rear windows, the security escort came for me. We checked, as always, at the charge office before going up. We meandered through the merciless corridors to the lifts. When we reached the Tenth Floor, I was led through the long passage into an office.

Inside two officers were chatting. One left as soon as the escort dumped me there.

'I'm Major Malan,' said the other, shaking my hand. (What was going on? – he was shaking my hand!) 'I come from Brixton Police Station. I am actually from Kliptown, but am relieving someone at Brixton.' Major Malan, tall and wearing a blue suit, had been sent to investigate the assault case. 'But unfortunately,' he said, 'the statement you made is lost. Do you mind making another one?' I didn't. We went over the matter all over again. But nothing happened. I'm still waiting.

With its stark bestiality, detention was hard. We were not really surprised when some detainees died. Indeed, the first couple of days of detention are crucial. If you survive them, the chances are you'll pull through. Dumisani Mbatha, a Soweto teenage boy, died soon after his detention on 16 September. So did Mapetla Mohapi, Jacob Mashobane, Luke Mazwembe and a host others. They were not the first to die in the abyss. Nor would they be the last. In virtually all cases, police had stock answers to queries. The detainees, they assured the nation, either hanged themselves or died when they fell down steep stairways or jumped to their deaths through windows. Yet we were guarded everywhere except when locked up in the cells. Always armed, the African security policemen hovered around everywhere: in interrogation rooms, the charge office where we had to make entries whenever we went out of or returned to the cells, and in the shower rooms. In fact, they had no other job, it seemed. And we had been stripped of all dangerous weapons – belts and even nail clippers. But we died all the same. The death toll grew alarmingly, people whose bodies had been broken, battered, crushed. I have a terrifying feeling that I would have become just one of the many statistics of detention 'suicides' or 'accidents' had I not regained consciousness on that fateful Thursday afternoon on 29 July.

CHAPTER 8

THE CRY FOR LAND

The noonday was bright and cool on Saturday, 21 November. I sat with some friends under a peach tree in the backyard at 586A Mahume Street in Naledi, celebrating my release the day before. Everybody seemed excited, as if I had risen from the dead. People had been coming in and out since early that morning. Some young children romped the street singing:

> *Tsietsi le Vorster*
> *Ba ngola teste;*
> *Vorster ke setlaela,*
> *Tsietsi o phasitse.*

> *(Tsietsi and Vorster*
> *They write a test*
> *Vorster is stupid*
> *Tsietsi has passed.)*

They stood holding hands in a circle, then moved clockwise as they chanted the first two lines and anti-clockwise when chanting the last two, dancing.

Tsietsi Mashinini, a former member of the Student Christian Movement, head prefect and science student at Morris Isaacson High school, was well-known among students through the townships. Christened Donald by his parents and their church, he discarded that name in 1972 in favour of Tsietsi, his African family name, after being influenced by Saso, the Black Consciousness student organisation. The youth considered him some sort of beacon of hope. They adored and respected his uncompromising stand against the system, his fearlessness and commitment. Although he was said to be far from being the best student in his class, he had always shone with confidence and forthrightness in debates in which he regularly represented his school. Besides, all were aware of his outspoken leadership. Older people within the community did not know him and the few who claimed to have known him even before 16 June considered him somewhat impetuous.

The idea of a student march into the heart of Johannesburg, which had been simmering despite total unease among parents, had crystallised soon after the Soweto Students Representative Council (SSRC) was formed – with Tsietsi Mashinini at the helm – at the end of July. In traditional fashion, the kids dubbed their leader *Naman'e Tshehla* (Grey Calf), revealing their high esteem for the freckle-faced young man from Central West Jabavu.

Even though students already had Sasm in existence, the leadership knew it did not enjoy the support of all high school children. Also, it had been inactive and had never really concerned itself with matters outside school. They felt there was a need for a new body, for them to be able to utilise all the manpower at their disposal. Thus the SSRC was formed to formulate, direct and articulate students' demands and grievances. Not only were they mad with Afrikaans, as had been the reason for the protest march on 16 June. They now wanted the Verwoedian system of education scrapped and the regional education directors, Ackerman and his circuit inspector, thrown out of Soweto. *'Sikhalela izwe lethu* – we demand our land back,' they cried, which meant they now sought total freedom; not just universal education, but freedom to live as human beings as well. They wanted to be accorded full citizenship and respect. They rejected all forms of oppression and exploitation inherent in the apartheid system. *'Sikhalela izwe lethu.'* The chant resounded with anger and self-pity, but the kids had added elements of pride, self-love and respect as they chanted down the streets. Parents heard passionate voices as Tsietsi and his lieutenants combed schools organising the proposed march. But would they heed the call for them to throw in their lot? Tsietsi had been on the run from police for almost a month now, but it was still his task to mobilise the forces. His immediate problem was that some students were staying away from school. And he wanted them back. Not so much to study, but rather to urge them to support the march.

Once again, the school children streamed back into the streets on Wednesday, 4 August 1976, chanting, 'What have we done to deserve all this? Release the detainees. We are marching, not fighting.' They strutted in many large groups from various parts of the townships, heading towards town. There, they protested against the continued detention of some of their leaders. A sprinkling of adults, most of them women, joined their ranks. *Rand Daily Mail* reporter Gabu Tugwana described the scene the next morning:

> *At 11am yesterday the main column of demonstrators marched along the Soweto freeway singing freedom songs. A roadblock manned by seven black policemen carrying revolvers allowed them to pass. But the column – about 20 000-strong – had walked only two kilometres when it come face to face with armoured police land rovers and trucks under the railway bridge between New Canada rail station and Mzimhlophe Township. Only about 200 continued, shouting 'peace, we're not fighting but marching.' Police in camouflage uniforms jumped down and formed a cordon across the road. A police officer addressed the marchers through a police interpreter:*
>
> *'I want to assure you that we, the police, are not against your march,' he said. But do it the right way. You must throw away all the bottles and stones in your hands an keep out of*

the road to allow traffic easy passage. Then you will be allowed to pass.

The protesters, largely students, complied and marched on. They had walked barely 200 metres when a police 'hippo' truck approached. Teargas canisters were thrown. Students scattered. They re-assembled five minutes later, but had not walked more than 50 metres when another 'hippo' approached them near the Noordgesig traffic lights. The remaining protesters dispersed.

The Orlando bottle store near Noordgesig was on fire. Ten minutes later, police were on the scene. In another ten minutes a fire engine arrived. It was manned by an all-black crew. Onlookers jeered the firemen. They were ordered to leave immediately. At 12.10pm onlookers jeered a policeman guarding the scene of the fire. He opened fire with what looked like a machine-gun firing just above the heads of onlookers. No one was injured. A helicopter, hovering above the crowd, ordered all police to reinforce the New Canada bridge beyond Noordgesig where students had assembled. At 1.40pm the students started making their way through the mine dumps in an attempt to reach John Vorster Square. Hippos were driven into the veld and students driven back with teargas.

While police focused their attention on the marchers, a band of students led by Tsietsi quietly moved within Soweto, burning policemen's homes. They singled out security police sergeants Caswell Mokgoro, Benjamin Letlake and a Criminal Investigation Department (CID) policeman known as Hlubi. Their homes were set alight with petrol after family members had been cleared out. Mokgoro and Letlake, who worked at John Vorster, have since moved lock, stock and barrel out of Soweto. The day ended with five persons dead and thirteen wounded; a train set ablaze at

Westgate station (each coach adjoining the driver's cabin gutted); a rail signal box at Mzimhlophe damaged and a Johannesburg-bound train from Naledi stoned, windows smashed and the driver saved by the steel mesh grill covering the cabin.

Police put a price on Tsietsi's head. They offered a reward of R500 to anyone who could tell where he was hiding in order to arrest him. That was barely twenty-four hours after they had appealed to him to hand himself over to them because, they claimed, mobsters wanted to kill him. It was apparent that police were trying to hoodwink him into believing that they wanted to protect him, but the lad was not fooled. However, the R500 offer might have become the magic wand in a society wallowing in poverty and teeming with informers. Wouldn't some residents who knew have been tempted to tell the cops? There was general fear that the boy would be arrested. But events, it seemed, had knitted Soweto together; a solid spirit of unity had filtered into the community. Beaming with delight, Tsietsi's lieutenants ridiculed the police and their appeal. Instead of worrying about Tsietsi, they said, the police ought to be more concerned about the blood of their brothers and sisters who died from police bullets. Anyway, Tsietsi did not want any police protection in preventive detention. He was quiet safe in one of their friendly brother countries.

Through the help of other people the fugitive had reached Gaborone and so dashed whatever hopes police had of catching him. Tsietsi was gone, leaving Khotso Seatlholo, a student from Naledi High, and other leaders in the midst of a massive campaign. They were still printing and distributing leaflets, urging parents to use the only weapon they had – withdrawal of their labour from industry, even though they knew that to do so was frowned upon by the laws of the country.

Embittered by the continued shootings and detentions, workers heeded the call. The kids had become a force, their influence almost total. They had demonstrated their own personal courage and the fact that through unity nothing was impossible. More than a million Soweto residents were astir on 24 August, and workers duly stayed away from work. Johannesburg was paralysed. The hardest hit was the clothing industry. All but a few factories were closed in the absence of the traditional cheap labour force. White, coloured and Indian workers, who reported for work, were consequently sent home. Soweto was mystified when after nightfall thousands of migrant labourers from Mzimhlophe Hostel attacked families in the neighborhood.

Banded into an impi and armed with sticks, assegais and pangas, the hostel-dwellers broke into homes, beating up inhabitants and breaking up furniture. Scores of women were raped. But police were indifferent to the attacks, and residents claimed that the police had actually incited the labourers, whose families lived in the homelands, to attack them. However, their claims were repudiated by the police. The police commissioner said he had no knowledge of the 'rampaging Zulus'. But if it had happened, he was not surprised. People, he said, were getting tired of the things that were happening in Soweto. Zulus had been harassed, attacked and their homes burnt down. They were simply reacting to the harm done to them. They had organised themselves and had every right to do so.

It was a startling statement. There had never been any organised attacks on hostel-dwellers, nor did hostel-dwellers have any homes in Soweto to be burnt by demonstrators. And what made it even more revealing was that when Gibson Thula, the KwaZulu envoy in the Reef, appealed to hostel inmates for calm, he was stopped and summoned to Protea where he was given a message from the Minister of Police. Thula was ordered not to interfere in the troubled hostel nor interfere with police actions. Police, he was told, knew what they were doing and their task should not be made more difficult. Understandably, Soweto was enraged. Some residents later attacked the hostel and killed four inmates after the hostel men had molested a motorist, burning his car.

Despite their knowledge that other ethnic groups also stayed in the hostel, police authorities and the Minister of police put the emphasis on Zulus in an attempt to make people believe the student unrest had turned into a fight, with Zulus standing on the side of the police. But they were not successful. Chief Mangosuthu Buthelezi, who personally intervened despite opposition from the minister, denounced as untrue that Zulus had attacked the people of Soweto.

Within weeks Soweto kids were singing, 'Tsietsi and Vorster are writing a test.' Accompanied by two fellow students, Barney Mokgatle and Selby Selema, the SSRC secretary and treasurer respectively, the highly sought-after fugitive had reached London. Through press conferences, he spoke to the world, stressing that black South Africans wanted 'absolute power now'; that they were no longer interested in having 'equal rights' with whites who, he said, had 'created all the bitterness' within the country. He also urged foreign companies doing business in South Africa to get out in compliance with calls for sanctions.

The hostel-dwellers, there were 45 000 of them throughout Soweto, were a people apart. If Soweto officially comprised a second-class people, the hostel-dwellers must have constituted a third-class community. Their living conditions were squalid and they had no rights whatsoever. Perhaps they could boast only of the right, if it must be called a right, to work and live in Johannesburg, away from their families. They were not even entitled to proper housing and therefore had to live in the hostels. Each hostel consisted mainly of a block of dwellings or halls and each hall was divided into four tiny blocks, housing a total of sixteen persons, each on his own bed. There was one large concrete table and a small stove for heating in each hall for the inhabitants. They stored their foodstuffs and, using primus stoves, cooked and ate within the halls. Often their clothes hung on wires and strings below the rafters. Common water taps were provided outside the halls. So were toilets and showers, rows upon rows of unpartitioned sewerage and urinals and shower taps housed within open halls. Here, privacy was a luxury, something unknown. With no recreational facilities available, the hostel-dweller spent all his leisure time in the beer-hall in an attempt to kill boredom.

Conditions within the hostels encouraged sexual infidelity. Hostel-dwellers engaged in homosexual acts and often lured young girls into their rooms for sex. In that way the hostels promoted, albeit unwittingly, a breakdown both in parental authority in homes in the townships and the break-up of marriages, not only in the townships but in the so-called homelands as well. But relations between the people of Soweto and the hostel-dwellers had always been relatively good. The people had so far never considered each other as enemies. They were, strictly speaking, brothers and sisters with more than the oppressive system as the basis of their affinity.

It was not until 23 September 1976 that students actually surprised Johannesburg. For the first time in the history of South Africa, black children – some armed with petrol bombs, stones and knives – marched through the city centre. It was another crippling blow to the country's economy, and the worst industrial disruption for decades. Mingling with workers, they had come into town by bus, taxi and train. They then gathered outside the Johannesburg Railway Station. It was about 8am when business opened. Shopkeepers, stunned, stood around and watched as students unfurled banners and started singing 'This is our country'.

But the singing throng was intercepted. It was still marching down Eloff Street, approaching the city centre, when police arrived. They sealed off the area. Firemen watched the marchers as police confronted them. Hell broke loose, with police opening fire and children exploding their homespun petrol bombs. Several whites still on the way to work were trampled and stabbed by fleeting crowds.

Then hundreds of black workers congregated in Kerk Street.

Four police vehicles pulled up. The police climbed out of their vehicles and attacked the crowd with batons. Ambulances took the injured to hospital and many blacks, most of them young, were arrested. They were bundled into police vehicles and driven away. Police attitudes hardened considerably after the march. They opened fire even at cemeteries where residents buried the dead. At least four people were fatally shot and about fifty others wounded during the burial of Jacob Mashobane and Anna Mkwanazi (both children who died in detention).

The Pelican Nightclub, a shebeen in Orlando East, was rocked by a bomb explosion at the end of November. There was a similar attack on a house in Mapetla on 7 November, and on the Jabulani Police Station on 24 October. Police arrested Paul Mangaliso Langa, aged twenty-eight, in connection with the bomb explosions. He was subsequently tried and convicted on charges under the Terrorism Act. The judge said it had been the intention of Langa and his accomplices to kill the police on duty at Jabulani. Only chance had prevented the bomb from being placed in the envisaged position. The South African police, he said, were part of the administration of law and order and were in the front line in the maintenance of the authority of the state. He had considered the death penalty but a number of factors, including luck, had seen to it nobody had been killed in the explosion. Leaders of greater authority in the students movement had been in South Africa at the time and, possibly, with Langa when the explosion occurred. But the exact part played by him in the explosion had not been proved, except that he was the leader of the 'suicide squad' of the SSRC.

He sentenced him to twenty-five years in prison.

The Pelican and Mapetla houses were apparently bombed when owners overlooked students appeals not to sell liquor. Students wanted shebeens to identify themselves with the struggle by abstaining from selling drinks.

At about noon on 7 December, a former student of the

University of the Witwatersrand, Isaac Seko, exploded a bomb in front of the Boulevard Restaurant at the Carlton Centre. His right hand was blown off in the explosion. Several people in the restaurant were injured. Seko, twenty five years old, was arrested. Three days later police also arrested Wellington Tshazibane, an Oxford University graduate in engineering. Tshazibane died hours after his detention. Seko was tried and convicted at a special court in Springs. Police claimed during his trial that he had been trained by Tshazibane in the use of explosives and that he had bombed a white doctor's surgery at Klipspruit on 5 November.

Seko told the court he had thrown the bomb he had made into the surgery to test its usefulness. What he did, he said, was with the highest patriotic motives for the good of his people and, he believed, for the good of white South Africa as well. He exploded the bombs to shake authorities into effecting meaningful reforms to improve living conditions in Soweto, which, he said, was like a prison turned into a battle ground. Until 16 June, he said, he had never supported any political organisation. He had taken no interest in black or white politics. Police had attacked, killed and injured many young people – mainly school children – involved in a peaceful protest. That clearly brought home to him the unfairness of the apartheid system. Then he decided to use his skills to produce inflammable devices to help students fight against authorities.

The last straw, he said, was in October. He was attending the funeral of Jacob Mashobane who died in detention. Hundreds had gathered around the graveside. Several cars drove up and police alighted from the cars; triggers were pulled. People scattered whilst others were brought down – some dead, some wounded. Those who managed to scale the fence were gunned down by a contingent outside the cemetery. As the crowd scattered, he and a few other people remained standing. They were forced at gunpoint to carry the dead and injured into the cars and vans nearby. Seko believed blacks were born again on 16 June. Their single objective was a ruthless spirit of loathing and rage against white South Africa. No army could withstand the strength of an idea whose time had come, he wrote in his diary which was read in court during his trial. He was sentenced to twelve years for terrorism for the Carlton Centre blast; seven years for sabotage for the Klipspruit surgery attack and five years for possession of explosives. However, all three jail terms were to run concurrently. That meant Seko would spend only twelve years in prison, not the total of twenty-four years.

By then 400 people had died in Soweto alone since 16 June, according to press reports. Two hundred children had fled from the area to neighboring Botwsana and Swaziland, and more than 200 others, including Motlana, Winnie Mandela and Mathlare (the BPA leaders), had been detained. A strange virus had also hit Soweto. Numerous people were developing sores and itchy eyes. Some were becoming blind, some semi-blind. Most were children in their teens. Some were taken to St John's Eye Hospital at the bottom of Baragwanath. But others simply suffered from within the confines of their homes. What evil had befallen the settlement? Far too many were being detained and lying in detention. Now the mystery disease; no one could tell what the matter really was and doctors were not telling either. The kids had never suffered from eye problems before. But they had one thing in common – they had all been shot at. Some were shot in clashes between police and students, some had been shot as they walked home after school or as they romped about on pavements and in open spaces within the townships.

Lena Monamodi, a nine-year-old girl, was completely blind when she was taken to St John's where she underwent four operations. The little girl had been walking in the street when a policeman allegedly shot her in the face. She collapsed and the car sped away. Longsdale Kananda, aged fourteen, was on the way home from school with several other children when police in a truck allegedly fired at them, hitting him in the eye. His eye was removed. Joseph Norexe, another fourteen-year old, was also hit in the face. He was completely blinded. Yet another schoolboy, Reginald Mhkize, aged eighteen, became victim of the blind shots too. Although he could still see, he was partially paralysed. But Johannes Dube, seventeen years old, totally lost his sight after police allegedly peppered him with the pellets. He was a pupil at Dr Vilakazi Secondary School in Zola. He was with a friend, Thomas Malaza, when they were attacked during school break. They were walking towards the taxi rank; a police car, lime-green, stopped near them. The children were ordered to stop and they obeyed. One of the policemen pulled out a gun. He allegedly fired at the two boys, hitting Thomas Malaza in the leg. Johannes, frightened, began screaming. More shots rang out. He was hit on his head, the side of his body and in his eye.

But for the grace of God, these absurdities would never had come to light had a doctor at St John's, obviously disgusted by the callousness of the police in dealing with children, not spoken out. The doctor (he never disclosed his name) said he had treated several black children blinded by birdshot during the disturbances. The children were, on average, twelve years old. Some had permanently injured eyesight. The trouble with birdshot, he explained, was that it sprayed and that was where the danger of blinding came in. He felt some of the affected children could have been mere bystanders, watching whatever was going on, at the time they were shot. The most frightening thing, however, was not so much what the doctor revealed, but rather the attempt by authorities to hush things up. The deputy commissioner of police in charge of riot police said that police could not fire deliberately at anyone's eye, but anything, even sand, could blind.

Both the director of hospital services in the Transvaal and the Baragwanath Hospital superintendent would not talk. The hospital superintendent said he would not disclose information about the victims who had been treated without permission (!). But the Johannesburg-based *Sunday Times* did reveal that police had been using birdshot in controlling riots for several months. Jimmy Kruger, the Minister of Justice and Police, had earlier told the newspaper that birdshot was the answer in dealing with rioters. He said that birdshot was safe, more effective than rubber bullets and not as lethal as ordinary bullets. Of course, we now know better.

CHAPTER 9

THE RENT ISSUE

The new year was barely seven days old when the townships were rocked by a bomb blast on 7 January. That night a group of elderly Soweto residents, some of them migrant labourers who lived in the hideous hostels dotted all over the ghetto, had gathered in a house at Klipspruit. Police have said the group was making bombs and that one of the bombs exploded. Several of the men were injured and the house partially destroyed. At least seven of the men were arrested and detained. Led by one of the detainees, police later recovered ammunitions or caches of arms buried in backyards in some homes. Elmond Malele, one of the men, died in detention shortly after they were picked up. The six others were charged under the Terrorism Act.

The BPA was in total disarray despite the fact that all but one of its leaders, Mokoena, had been released from detention. But the SSRC still reigned supreme in the life of the townships. It had gained enormous power and influence in the last five months of 1976, directing thought and successfully organising strikes and burying victims of the unrest. The movement seemed to have the capacity to adapt to the effects of detention, either under Section 6 of the Terrorism Act or the Internal Security Act, the laws that gave police the right to take people into custody merely because they may have become potential witnesses in future trials or were considered a threat to the security of the state. Even the large-scale exodus of students fleeing the country into exile did not seem to affect its activities. However, when *The World* newspaper published an illustrated story that fugitive SSRC president Khotso was wounded in a brush with the security police, it seemed cops were closing in on the movement and that it would be crippled. The fugitive had encountered the police while travelling in a car and they had opened fire, hitting him in the arm. He escaped and disappeared completely from the scene thereafter.

Soweto children wasted no time in choosing a successor. But Daniel Montsisi, a somewhat frail, bashful and soft-spoken young man from Sekano-Ntoane, did not have the charisma of any of his predecessors. However, he seemed to have accepted his new position with equal enthusiasm, dedication and preparedness. The children gave him due respect, unqualified support. The quality of his leadership was soon to be tested.

No sooner had he ascended to the throne than the West Rand Administration Board, a branch of the government entrusted with the administration of the townships, proposed to raise house rents by as much as fifty per cent in some cases. The board claimed it had to increase the rents because it had no funds as its main source of revenue, the numerous bottle stores, had been destroyed during the uprising on 16 June. It had since been running Soweto at a loss, and there was a breakdown in services. It, therefore, had to raise the rent charges in order to be able to continue supplying the much-needed services. (Urban Africans in South Africa must be the only people in the world who have to drink liquor in order to maintain services within their own areas.) Basically, the board wanted to punish inhabitants for the riots, and they were understandably outraged.

When accused of planning to raise rents without even having had the decency to consult residents, officials of the board claimed they had held meetings with the Urban Bantu Council (UBC), the puppet African advisory body which was imposed on the people by the government in 1968 to serve as their official link between Soweto and the government. The board also claimed that council members had approved the proposal to increase rents. This, however,

Hector Pieterson, first victim of 1976 shootings,
carried by Soweto pupil, Mbuyisa Makhubu,
for emergency medical assistance.
He was certified dead at the local clinic.
(Photo/Sam Nzima)

Sam Nzima. (Photo/The Star)

Protestors on 16 June, 1976 (Photo/The Star)

16 June 1976 riots (Photo/IMAGES24.co.za)

Tsietsi Mashnini (left), a student leader during the time of the 1976 riots (Photo/Alf Khumalo)

Soweto youths kneel in front of police, showing the peace sign, 1976 (Photo/IMAGES24.co.za)

Desmond Tutu
(Photo/Alf Kumalo)

Onkgopotse Abram Tiro, a student leader at
Turfloop, gave an address to a graduation
ceremony slamming Bantu Education. He was
killed in Botswana, 1974, by a parcel bomb.
(Photo/Alf Kumalo)

The author, with a
neck brace, after his
experiences in detention.
(Photo/Alf Kumalo)

Mrs Winnie Mandela, wife of imprisoned African National Congress leader, Nelson Mandela in their house in Orlando West Soweto. (Photo/Alf Kumalo)

Steve Biko, founding father of the Black Consciousness philosophy in South Africa, died in detention on 12 September 1977. (Photo/Alf Kumalo)

Nengwekhulu and Tiro (Photo/Alf Kumalo)

Mr Mangaliso Robert Sobukwe, the President of the Pan-Africanist Congress (Photo/Sam Nzima)

Protests in Soweto, 1976. (Photo/The Star)

Protestors in 1976 (Photo/IMAGES24.co.za)

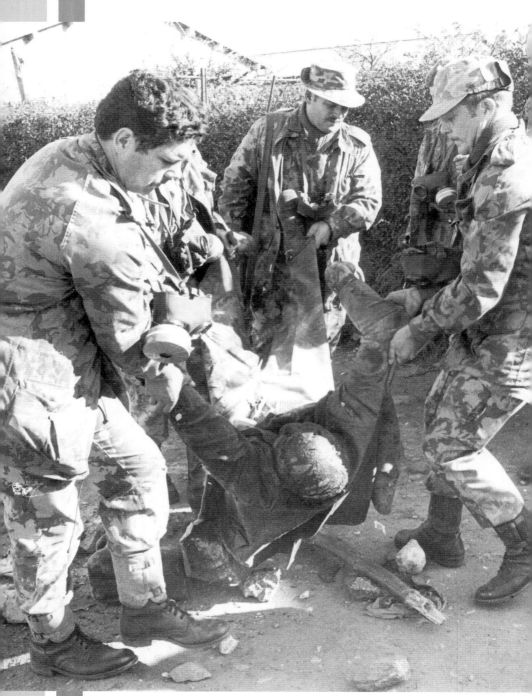

Policemen carrying a protestor during the 1976 riots (Photo/The Star)

was denied by the councillors. Officials, they said, had merely told them the rents would be raised and had not even given them the chance to discuss the matter. However, residents were sceptical, and whatever credibility councillors might have had among some residents, especially adults, was damaged beyond repair.

The SSRC, whose members had variously ridiculed the UBC as a 'Useless Boys Club' and a castrated bull, went for the kill. Through their leaders, the children argued that parents were too poor and could not afford the new rents. They urged parents to hold public meetings to demonstrate their opposition. They called upon council members to resign. And when it seemed the councillors were not taking them seriously, the SSRC executive visited some individual councillors at their homes, putting pressure on them to do so. Several community leaders, who were not connected with the council, supported the stand taken by the student organisation. Perhaps in an attempt to save face, David Thebehali, the council chairman, flew to the United States where, on his return, he claimed to have raised a R217 million loan for the administration of the ghetto. No details were given. Thebehali found that most of his councillors had resigned during his visit abroad. Soon after his return, the SSRC held a boycott of classes in protest against the proposed rent hikes. On the morning of the demonstration, Daniel Montsisi issued a press statement to *The World,* giving an assurance that the protest would be peaceful.

Students converged on an open ground at the bottom of Elkah Stadium in Rockville. He joined them later, after returning from his press conference. He once again warned the assembled throng against violence. But there was tension in the air as the thousands of children, singing, slowly advanced to the road above the stadium, where a contingent of police stood waiting. Still at a distance from the armed police, the crowd, now silent, stopped moving. Three youngsters, apparently some of his lieutenants, broke out of the mob. With their hands raised as if surrendering themselves, they advanced haltingly towards the police; then they stopped halfway and knelt down, still with their hands held high. After what seemed a moment, they rose and moved closer, only to stop once more, kneeling again.

They then beckoned the police officer, Major Malan, who stood in front of the contingent, to meet them. A grim–faced old man broke away from the small crowd of onlookers. He joined the three kneeling boys. He also knelt behind them and, unlike them, seemed to be praying. As Major Malan, his rifle in hand, strode towards them, one of the three boys quickly dropped his hands, rose up and retreated. But the others held on. They frantically waved at the police officer, pleading with him to leave his rifle behind. The officer swung round. He handed his rifle to some other policeman. Then the apprehensive youngster got back to his place. Major Malan joined them and squatted. They shook hands with him. They told him that students would not make trouble. They only wanted to march peacefully to the UBC chambers. They begged him not to allow his men to shoot. His men, he assured them, would not touch the students if they behaved. But he warned the boys there might be *tsotsis* (thugs) in their ranks bent on causing trouble and that if there was any trouble his men would not hesitate to shoot.

There was a sign of relief as the group rose and the officer returned to the police and the boys to the crowd. A roar of 'Amandla Awethu' rent the air. The old man, now grinning, shuffled back to the onlookers crowded on the roadside. Led by the boys, the children trotted, like an army of ants, through the stadium. They got onto the road, leaving the police behind, marched up the street towards the UBC there, to present their demands to the chairman of the council. In vain they waited for him on the lawn outside the building. By early afternoon, they were still waiting. One of the leaders said he feared there would be trouble if a bread or milk delivery vehicle were to get anywhere near the children. They were hungry and tired, he said, because they had had nothing to eat since sunrise. However, he said his colleagues would still do their best to maintain order. A white cameraman, who had been sitting on the step of the UBC building, disappeared into the chamber. Then he emerged on the balcony above and began taking pictures of the crowd below. Someone threw an empty bottle at him, but it crashed on the wall. Suddenly some students stormed the building, smashing windows. Others fled in all directions, running away from the scene. The children had broken their side of the agreement with the police. About five schoolboys were arrested in connection with the day's disturbances later that evening. But the case against them was eventually dropped.

It was clear that the council would never be the same again. The children had forcefully demonstrated their opposition to it. Thebehali, accompanied by councillors Richard Maponya and Tolica Mkhaya, former chairman, visited Cape Town where they had an audience with the minister of Bantu Administration, MC Botha. After their meeting, the minister announced that he was suspending the proposed rent increases. A few days later the three councillors also announced their resignation from the council, signaling the collapse of the apartheid institution. Whatever doubts still lingered over the power wielded by the children were dispelled.

Hopes that schooling would return to normal in Soweto in 1977 were dashed by sporadic disruptions after the new academic year began. The children were continuing the fight for a better education system, for a political dispensation. But there was still the paradox. In Diepkloof, students of Namedi Junior Secondary, a school that for years had existed in name only, had now taken it upon themselves the responsibility of erecting the school building. They were tired, they said, of being without a school of their own, and being housed in other schools. They hired and showed films to raise funds to build the school. They appealed to charitable institutions and to industry for help, to augment the pittance they collected from shows. Furthermore, most students were keen to write the belated end-of-year exams in March. But their leadership floundered when they announced that students would not write. On whose behalf was the executive now talking? Some students repudiated the announcement. They accused the leadership of no longer serving their interests. A division among students had arisen. Education authorities tried to exploit the chasm within the student council. They claimed that the president was not a student, and that he was too old, in fact he had long ago dropped out of school. But the trick did not work. Students eventually wrote the examinations. Daniel Montsisi remained head of the SSRC.

Surprisingly, students fared unusually well in examinations in March despite the fact that there hadn't been much schooling since the start of the revolt the previous June. Schools produced more first-class passes than at any other time in the history of Soweto. Furthermore, there was an almost one hundred per cent pass rate throughout the townships. But the results were greeted with jeers by educationists. They said that standards were deliberately lowered in an apparent move to win children off the streets back into the classrooms.

CHAPTER 10

UNDETERRED

In its own niggardly way, the government stirred. Compulsory teaching in Afrikaans was suspended indefinitely. Ackerman was thrown out of the region that included Soweto, and so was De Beer, the school inspector. School children were promised a better deal two years from then, when they would be given free textbooks. There were other promises too, including the introduction of service training for teachers. Teachers would also be encouraged to study through correspondence with government itself providing study grants to enhance the quality of teaching. The name Bantu Education would be abandoned for the simple reason that it was 'offensive' to blacks. (Had the government at long last realised that even the oppressed resented insults?) Otherwise, conditions remained just as they had always been – rigid as ever.

Schools would still be ethnically divided, and children reaching the age of seventeen still had to apply for passes or reference books even though they were still at school. In making those applications they had to declare their tribal origins; where their fathers were born, not where they themselves were born, so that their citizenship could be established, for black people could only be citizens of Bantu Homelands, not South Africa. Then they would be subjected to the provisions of the Bantu (Urban Areas) Consolidation Act of 1945 as amended by the Bantu Laws Amended Act of 1964. Section 10(1)(b) of the Act stipulated that 'no Bantu (African) shall remain for more than seventy-two hours in a prescribed area unless he produced proof that (a) he has since birth resided continuously in such an area for a period of not less than fifteen years and has not, during either period or after, been sentenced to a fine exceeding one hundred rand or imprisonment for a period exceeding six months.'

For practical purposes it meant, among other things, that an African still had to check documents of the woman he wanted to marry before committing himself to make sure, absolutely sure, she was someone legally safe to love. Choosing the wrong wife or rather the wife with wrong qualifications could land him in unending homelessness, for only couples with proper qualifications were eligible for housing. The magic qualifications were all contained in the Bantu (Urban Areas) Consolidation Act, the law governing a black man's right, and that of his spouse, to live in a prescribed urban area. Without the passbook, Africans still risked arrest and they could not seek work nor rent houses, register births and deaths without it.

In short, the status quo remained intact.

Inhabitants, especially the young, were unmoved. The SSRC called on members to boycott the end of the year examinations. It also declared the Christmas season a period of mourning for all those who died since the upheavals of 16 June. The leadership said students could not be expected to write when they had been unable to study because of the crisis facing schools in particular and the black community generally. Although some students were keen to write, all attempts by education authorities to hold examinations failed. It seemed even those students who wanted to write feared to be seen doing so, and they stayed away from exam centres. Still expressing student opposition to Bantu Education generally, the leadership argued that the type of education they received was a poison destroying their minds, killing their sense of creativity, frustrating them. It was designed to make them slaves in their own country, and they rejected it in its entirety.

The black masses were urged not to celebrate in any way for the festive season, specifically to abstain from selling and drinking liquor, and not to buy new clothes. No food parcels from the city were to be brought into Soweto. Food had to be bought from township stores only. Those who tried to flout the appeal had their articles destroyed or their shebeens attacked. And there were some casualties.

Soweto was still recovering from the shock of yet another death in detention, that of Tshazibane, the only black engineering graduate in the area, if not throughout the country, on 10 December. Percy Qoboza, the editor of *The World* newspaper, was detained five days later. His home had been raided at about 3.30am. His arrest once again showed that the police wanted to intimidate the press, to stop the black masses from knowing what was happening in their communities, what the police themselves were doing to the people. Earlier attempts – with the detention of many black journalists who were covering the continuing upheavals and shootings – had not been successful. Police had now gone, as it were, for the big fish: the only black editor in Johannesburg whose white-owned newspaper enjoyed the support of the black people. There was a deafening outcry from his colleagues. He was released about eight hours after his arrest, after questioning. Police had detained him, they said, because they had believed he had information on fugitive student leaders.

By some coincidence, the marathon Saso/BPC trial which, in essence, was the trial of the philosophy of Black Consciousness, ended that day, when the nine accused were found guilty under the Terrorism Act. Moves to cripple the Black Consciousness movement dated as far back as 1974, soon after Saso in conjunction with BPC organised the 'Viva Frelimo' rally to celebrate Mozambique's victory and independence from Portugal.

Jimmy Kruger had banned the rally in Durban but it took place anyway. Saso and BPC offices were subsequently raided, and many leaders detained. It was not until after nearly four months of incommunicado detention that nine of the leaders were brought to trial on 31 January 1975, on charges of violating the Terrorism Act. The charges related to the rallies, to Saso and BPC documents and to the theory of Black Consciousness itself. And a series of likely results of the men's actions which, unless disproved by the accused, presumed them guilty, were listed. There were no allegations of physical terrorism whatsoever. So the accused had to prove that their pamphlets, speeches and philosophy were not likely to embarrass government administration, promote general disorder and hostility between the races or endanger maintenance of law and order. The trial had dragged on for almost two years until that day – 15 December – when the nine accused were found guilty of committing acts capable of endangering maintenance of law and order.

Their conviction showed, clearly, that an individual could be found guilty under the Terrorism Act if it could be proved he had, or he failed to prove he did not have, an intention to endanger law and other. The judge ruled that neither Saso nor BPC had the characteristics of revolutionary groups. Although the object of the accused had been to achieve total liberation of blacks and to bring about total change in the political, social and economic systems of the country, they, unlike revolutionaries, had made use of rallies, demonstrations and strikes. Revolutionary groups, said the judge, organised secretly and usually planned to seize power through sabotage, terrorist tactics and armed action.

The judge claimed that all the accused felt that a grave injustice had been done to blacks by whites, that blacks were numerically superior, with an historical and natural right to rule the country. In their view, the judge went on, right had been usurped by whites who really had no business to be in South Africa. The whites clung tenaciously to their political power and privileged positions and had proved to be intransigent. Attempts to regain the alleged birthright of the blacks had failed. The accused believed that the reasons for the failures were that the blacks had not been properly motivated, that they were always divided and the whites succeeded in keeping them divided, that the blacks did not realise the extent of their own misery, the extent of crimes of whites, the potential power that was locked up in the black masses and the Utopia that could be gained by eliminating the whites, said the judge. They realised that political action was necessary to mobilise and prepare blacks and to involve them in a total struggle for a total change. That was to be achieved under the banner of Black Consciousness by means of conscientisation.

The judge said that the accused felt that blacks had to be made to realise the extent of their misery, that their present condition was a far cry from that which was theirs by right, that the source of their misery was the whites. Anything offered to blacks in the line of, for instance, political institutions, was in fact an effort to divide and rule so as to keep the blacks in perpetual servitude. There had to be a vision of the Utopia which would result from total change and that vision was of an open, egalitarian society, organised on a basis of black communalism (a concept of sharing). The judge also said Black Consciousness was an attitude of mind, which encouraged blacks to reject all value systems that sought to make them foreigners and reduce their basic human dignity. Cohesion and solidarity were important because Black Consciousness implied awareness by blacks of the power they wielded as a group, economically and politically. The practical effect of this was that specific language was used by the accused to condemn whites as the oppressors, and everything associated with whites, especially its institutions and the police. In the process, language was used which encouraged feelings of hostility where they did not exist, between blacks and whites. Blacks were persuaded that violence against whites, who were inherently violent and unjust, and had robbed the blacks of their heritage by force of arms, was necessary. All reasonable requests by blacks were cruelly suppressed by armed force and the whole system of government of whites was based on violence. Evidence showed that two people cited as co-conspirators, who were not charged, had opposed the holding of Frelimo rallies after they had been banned under the Riotous Assemblies Act, not because it was not the policy of BPC to go ahead when confrontation seemed inevitable, but because BPC was not yet ready for a violent confrontation. A violent confrontation was welcomed at Turfloop and in Durban. The organisers continued to hold the rallies despite the fact that they knew police were on the scene to prevent them. They expected and desired a violent confrontation. The accused decided upon and organised the holding of rallies to embarrass the government and to exploit the emotions which the success of Frelimo roused in the breast of the blacks, said the judge.

The accused – Saths Cooper, Muntu Myeza, Mosiuoa 'Terror' Lekota, Aubrey Mokoape, Nkwenkwe Nkomo, Pandelani Nefolovhodwe, Zithulele Cindi, Strini Moodley and Kaborane Sedibe – were sentenced to jail terms of five to six years. It was a lesson that all critics of the status quo who actively sought change, contravened in one way or another the Terrorism Act. But angry Soweto was undeterred. Students continued exhorting residents not to celebrate the forthcoming Christmas.

A day on which township people often lived it up, Christmas was also a moment to settle old scores which almost always resulted in numerous assaults and murders. Nevertheless, it was essentially a children's festival and parents, no matter how poor, went out their way to give the children a treat, usually in the form of good meals, new clothes and toys, often chosen by the children themselves. Township tradition demanded that children should choose whatever gifts they needed for Christmas and New Year. So they were always brought by mothers into the city for shopping. And on celebration day a sheep or goat would be slaughtered for the occasion. Meals were relatively sumptuous, comprising rice and meat and vegetables and home-made ginger beer. Not only for the family but for Christmas hunters or revellers as well. Traditionally, adults went on the binge while children settled down to the good meals or pranced about the settlement.

Thus the abstinence call cut deeply through convention, indicating just how serious the opposition to the powerful forces of repression was. Most residents heeded the call. Many white businesses in the city, dependent on black customers, were virtually crippled. They remained idle at a time when they usually made fortunes. Christmas day was the quietest ever. Most families went to church services; others either spent the day at home or went out picnicking.

The student's call had also succeeded in curbing crime, as only about seven persons were reported by police to have been murdered, a figure less than the average number of weekend killings during the year.

CHAPTER 11

BLUEPRINT REJECTED

Both Motlana and Winnie Mandela were released from detention after about two or three months. They were let out without any charges levelled against them. That meant that police attempts to substantiate the lies that the ANC had planned the riots had failed. They returned to their respective jobs. The Soweto medical practitioner was once again running his two surgeries, while Mandela had returned to her receptionist job in the city. For the first time in a year she was re-united with her two daughters, Zeni and Zindzi, who had come back from Waterford High School in Mbabane, Swaziland. They were now living with her. The BPA leaders seemed to be settling down. Everything seemed peaceful and quite until the Cillié Commission, the one-man judicial inquiry that was appointed by the government to probe into the student disturbances, resumed its session in Pretoria after a spell in the Cape. Some detainee from Soweto (Mr Justice Cillié ruled that his identity should not be disclosed) was claiming in his testimony to the commission that Winnie Mandela and Motlana had tried to kill him before his detention because they felt he knew too much, as he too had been part of the BPA leadership. Mandela, he said, had one day given him poisoned soft porridge, but he had refused to eat it. On the other hand, Motlana had attempted to kill him with injections. The inference was that they wanted to get rid of him because they did not trust him and so feared he would spill the beans. Exposing whatever plot they were supposed to be involved in. (Anybody who had closely watched events in Soweto must have found all this somewhat childish and laughable.) The mystery man also claimed that on several occasions while driving to his home late at night he had seen student leaders at the Mandela household (another proof that students were under her spell?). In other words, she was the instigator who had organised the riots. (The police had at last found someone who did not mind being used as a medium for channelling lies. But I still wondered why, with such evidence, they still wouldn't prosecute. Perhaps even they didn't quite believe their man.)

These were absurd allegations. They were so puerile that only the police must have gained some satisfaction. (Otherwise, they would have been ashamed to present him to the commission. However, human decency eventually prevailed. Motlana and Mandela successfully applied to the commission to test the outrageous testimony. Through a legal representative, they cross-questioned the not-so-mysterious mystery witness, and his wild testimony did not withstand the test. It was exposed for what it was: a tissue of lies.

Within a week or so after the rebuttal of the strange evidence, Matlhare was released from detention. He returned home to Soweto, but found his surgeries had been dynamited. (If he asked, as I did, the people living opposite the surgery in Naledi, he must have also been told the surgery was destroyed by men, some white, in camouflage dress.)

Other men, in similar dress, were also accused by residents of having burnt libraries at Naledi and Morris Isaacson high schools. It may not be clear why 'these men' attacked the surgery in Naledi (another was gutted also by unknown persons in Zola), but detainees knew that police believed the two schools were Communist cells. However, no one else, neither teachers nor pupils, let alone the community, knew of the two schools as such cells. They were not aware of those cells, if indeed they did exist.

Matlhare's release was soon followed by that of Mokoena. I

didn't see Mokoena until much later, when he had already married. But Motlana told me he went straight to his job as BCP field worker after his release. In other words, Mokoena had gone to provide relief to stricken victims of the unrest in Soweto. Motlana, who was among those involved in carrying out the relief services provided by BCP, said the organisation's work had grown so much that the need for another person to assist Mokoena had arisen.

The Sowetan medical practitioner and some public-spirited colleagues, operating under the umbrella of the BCP, had already established a people's clinic at the Methodist Church Youth Centre in Central West Jabavu. Sick people, including victims of unrest, gathered there on specific days for treatment. The doctors ran the clinic in turns. Charges were minimal. Besides the medical services, BCP also gave relief to the poor to enable them to buy food and pay house rents. Without such help, there wouldn't have been much hope for many a family. Comrade Aid Movement, a new body, assisted BCP in rendering the service. It had been formed by students specifically to raise money for the purpose of giving relief to the community. But the new body seemed to be operating on a shoe-string.

The forces of repression once again struck the Mandela home. A squad of twenty policemen, travelling in four cars, descended on the house early Monday morning on 16 May 1977.

A police truck followed from behind. It also parked alongside the yard. Winnie was served with a banning order and immediately banished to Brandfort, a bleak little town in the Orange Free State, South Africa's most *verkrampte* (conservative) province, where blacks were traditionally not allowed into white shops. They had to stand in queues outside and buy through tiny windows specially made for them on the side walls, whence they couldn't properly see the person to whom they handed their money, as they asked for what they required.

All her belongings and furniture were loaded into the truck and she was bundled out of Soweto, without any regard to what was to happen to her teenage children, and in spite of the fact that she was still planning the marriage of her older daughter, Zeni.

Zeni was forced to join her fiancé in Swaziland. Her mother and sister were driven, much against their will, to the loneliness called Brandfort. Winnie and daughter Zindzi suddenly found themselves in a miserable world. They were dumped in a bare, semi-detached cottage.

Brandfort, tiny and desolate, seemed the sort of place where virtually every visitor would turn out to be a wolf in sheep's clothing. Sensitive Winnie must have been aware of all that. The apparent intention was to crush her spirit. But Winnie was Winnie. She had shown resilience in past years and that was what made Soweto hopeful that she might survive even Brandfort. However, there was much fear for Zindzi. What would be the effects of this kind of solitary confinement on her? Would she have the strength to withstand the dead weight of loneliness?

That Zindzi, who had already abandoned school to keep her house-arrested mother company (yes, house-arrested because she had to remain home day and night) would cope with the sordid new condition was debatable. But there was no question she belonged to a tougher and more unyielding generation than that of her parents. Soweto youths had exemplified that. The youngsters, unlike parents, did not seem to have any respect for authority (their parents had obeyed white man's authority for a long time, but they would not). They viewed the government's homeland policy, for instance, with far greater hostility than their parents did. Furthermore, the events of the past years seemed to have made them more resolute to challenge the status quo.

Life went on just as precariously as it had since the previous June. Community leaders condemned the deportation of the Mandela family, but police did not lessen their activities in townships, even after her banishment. Relentlessly, they continued harassing residents generally and, in particular, hunting down the SSRC leadership. Sporadic disruption of classes also continued, with students some times staying out of school for fear of arrest in constant police raids. Also, they were speaking, through their leaders, of plans to celebrate the first anniversary of the upheavals of the previous June. The West Rand Administration Board, piqued by the enforced collapse of UBC, was also saying that community councils would be introduced to replace the dead UBC. Characteristically, the local authority or board was not consulting residents to check whether or not they accepted the new councils. After several months of concerted but abortive attempts to arrest the SSRC executive, security police detained Montsisi, the president, on Saturday, 11 June. A number of other officials of the organisation were also captured. They were meeting secretly in a private house in Diepkloof when the police pounced. The boys were immediately detained under Section 6 of the Terrorism Act. How did the police know of the secret meeting? Had the student movement been infiltrated? True, there had always been informers operating in the townships, but the SSRC had so far seemed a closely-knit organisation, enjoying support from the community. But then many students had been detained since the previous June and, some of them, released after brutal interrogation. It was also an open secret that the police had since the previous June been anxious to get, by hook or crook, knowledgeable people, especially among students themselves, to work for them. Had they now succeeded in their efforts? There was no way of knowing precisely, but suspicion that they had was very strong.

Two days later – on Monday, 13 June to be exact – three young Africans armed with guns shot dead two white men in Goch Street in Newtown, Johannesburg, almost a stone's throw from John Vorster Square, at about midday. Johannes Motloung, aged twenty, and twenty-one-year-old Solomon Mahlangu were soon arrested after a shoot-out with security police. A third man escaped. Security police claimed they were 'terrorists' and that they had received military training in Angola. They also said that the young men were some of the students who had fled into exile in 1976. Rife among black workers was the rumour that the young men were interrupted by a black taximan at Diagonal Street rank while trying to return to Soweto. The taximan, the rumour went, had refused to take them in his vehicle when he realised they were armed. They had then walked down Jeppe Street towards Fordsburg. In Goch Street they had attacked white workers at a store, killing the two whites. The incidents alarmed white Johanesburg incited and them to the wanton harassment of blacks.

Motloung and Mahlangu were charged with murder, with furthering the aims of the banned African Nation Congress and being in possession of weapons and ammunition. On their first appearance in court, the defence counsel said there had been only incoherent communication with Motloung. The counsel asked for an inquiry to determine whether Motloung was fit to stand trial. Medical evidence indicated that he had suffered head injuries, sustainining brain tissue damage in the process. In consequence, the young man had had great difficulty even in naming Mahlangu at a consultation with a specialist psychiatrist. His brain injury had resulted in deficient intellectual functioning memory. An district surgeon's report also revealed he had been confused and badly shocked when seen by the surgeon. The surgeon had also diagnosed a fractured jaw and skull. A assertion by his defence that he was not fit to stand trial was accepted.

After the detention of student leader Montsisi, another leader was appointed: Gordon 'Trofomo' Sono. Sono steered the boat. The anniversary commemoration was held as scheduled. For a week Soweto wore black in accordance with student demands. Services were held in many churches within the area at the end of the week. To mark the end of the celebrations, participants, most of them students, prayed and listened to protest poetry readings. They also sang freedom songs and watched dramatic sketches depicting the black man's experience. In some instances, the dramatics even simulated the shootings of the previous June and the subsequent uprising. Police broke up the services at the Anglican Church at Naledi. The assembled crowd was baton-charged and the cross above the altar ripped off.

Editor Percy Qoboza invited several individuals and leaders of respected organisations to an indaba towards the end of June. Among the organisations were BPC, BPA and the National Federation of Women. The response was overwhelming, and although Qoboza himself did not attend, the meeting was held in his office. Some school principals and shop-owners also attended. It was a representative meeting and its main decision was that the black community of Soweto desired to be granted municipal status so that it could run its own affairs, just as Johannesburg did. It also reiterated that UBC was totally unacceptable. A committee comprising ten members was elected, with Motlana as chairman. The committee was entrusted with the task of formulating a blueprint of how Soweto would be run. Other members of the committee were Sedupe Ramokgopa, businessman; Mathabane, Morris Isaacson High School principal; salesman Douglas Lolwane; Mashwabada Mayathula, minister of religion; Tom Manthata, BPC executive member; Thandisizwe 'Tizza' Mazibuko, BPC secretary general; Ellen Khuzwayo, Federation of Black Women executive member; Veli Kraai, shopowner; and Leonard Mosala, a former UBC member. Once finalised, the blueprint had to be presented to a residents' public meeting for approval. If accepted, negotiations with government would begin for its implementation.

Without delay, the Soweto Committee of Ten got down to business. Members felt Soweto should be divided into at least thirty wards. Each ward would elect a representative into a body that would run the townships once it had been declared a municipality with municipal powers. Needless to say, the elected candidates would constitute the true leaders, leaders respected by the community, and so fill the leadership vacuum.

However, everything was still subject to approval by the community. Once the governing body had been formed, the committee could cease to function. It seemed a considerably moderate proposal, the most moderate to come out of Soweto since the eruption of the upheavals. It indicated that at least the committee (and so the people if they accepted the blueprint) was prepared to negotiate with the government on how Soweto ought to be run and so, presumably, solve the crisis facing the country. In a way, it seemed to tie up with government policy that black people should control their own areas. But, alas, the government baulked. It rejected the committee outright.

The government's faithful servant, the West Rand Administration Board, claimed it was working with a committee of thirteen, representing the interest of the people of Soweto; the committee of thirteen would participate in the proposed community council. The logic, or should I say illogic, went something like this: if the people want a Committee of Ten, we'll do better with a committee of thirteen, who are even prepared to take part in a statutory body rejected by the community. But it was not really so surprising that the government turned down what seemed to be the wishes of people; that it wanted to go ahead with its own plans. After all, the black people had no vote, no power. Whites knew what was good for the Bantu! By trying to suggest what they wanted done, the African people were, in the eyes of the rulers, being uppity and this couldn't be allowed.

Consequently, the Committee of Ten never got the chance to present its proposals. Each time Motlana and his executive arranged a public meeting for residents, the all-powerful Jimmy Kruger banned it, claiming that the committee represented black power movements, not the people! In the end, it turned out that the committee of thirteen didn't exist, but the Committee of Ten was still barred from holding residents' public meetings. Indeed, the government frustrated the committee because it feared the people would endorse its proposals.

In yet another move reflecting the hardened attitude of the government, it was announced that forty post-primary schools in the townships were being taken over by the state. Pupils at the schools were asked to re-apply for admission, if they wished or wanted to continue schooling. Parents were asked to accompany them when and if they went to register. Otherwise, they would not be accepted. Regulations giving guidelines on admissions, suspension and expulsion were gazetted. They seemed to be aimed at dealing with the on-going school crisis. They provided for disciplinary action to be taken against pupils who 'harmed' the good name of the school, maintenance of order and discipline at school. Punishment included corporal punishment to boys, imposition of work, withholding privileges and expulsion. A maximum of four strokes either with cane or leather strap was prescribed; corporal punishment could be administered in case of gross neglect, truancy, disobedience, willful damage to property, flagrant lying, theft, dishonesty, assault, bullying and indecency. Students could also be suspended if a principal felt that their continued attendance would be detrimental to the welfare of the school. They would be considered expelled too if they were absent from school for five consecutive days without valid reasons from parents. Principals had to inspect attendance at least once a week and to ascertain reasons for absenteeism. Of course, neither parents nor students had been consulted in drawing up regulations.

The effects of the take-over of the schools were disastrous. Students refused to re-apply. The SSRC called on teachers to resign. For a while teachers continued reporting at school each day, but after a meeting at the Methodist Church Youth Centre where a teachers' action committee was formed, most teachers accepted the students call. At least 500 secondary school teachers resigned.

Thus schooling came to a standstill. Wittingly or unwittingly government had succeeded in paralysing education in Soweto.

No sooner had Mandela and her daughter arrived at Brandfort than they discovered that their cottage was under constant police surveillance. No relatives, let alone friends, could see the family without permission. Winnie had already been arrested and charged with breaking her banning order. Her trial was continuing. The situation was so hideous that teenage boys and girls who dared to visit Zindzi at her home were questioned and their individual friendships threatened.

By the last week of August the situation in the family was desperate. From Robben Island, Zindzi's father Nelson brought an urgent application in Bloemfontein Supreme Court against two security policemen who, he said in his affidavits, were terrorising his daughter. He wanted them restrained from interfering with personal friends and acquaintances at home and unlawfully harassing her for communicating with any of them. The Supreme Court was told the summary removal of Mrs Mandela from Orlando heralded a reign of terror by security police against her daughter. From the time she arrived in Brandfort, her newly-made friends were subjected to police harassment and intimidation; some were detained and interrogated. In one case, a friend was assaulted. Her loneliness and mental anguish were highlighted in a sworn statement from a psychiatrist and a general practitioner who had both treated her.

The interdict was granted, with cost to be paid by the police.

CHAPTER 12

STEVE BIKO

It was 12 September 1977. I rang Dr Nthato Motlana at his Diepkloof consulting rooms in Soweto, Johannesburg, a little before 11am. He was furious. 'Have you heard,' he asked as soon as he realised who it was. 'They've killed Steve Biko.'

'I was phoning to let you know.'

'And they want us to believe he starved himself to death.'

'It's a lie. I know Steve; he was a healthy, robust young man in the prime of his life.'

'Speaking as a doctor, I can tell you he would not have died even if he refused to eat for a month. What's seven days!'

'Yeah,' I said. 'We are running the story.'

Silence.

'Well, thanks for phoning. The overseas press is onto the story too. Some correspondents phoned earlier for comments,' he said.

We hung up.

My telephone rang as soon as I dropped the receiver. A female family friend was on the line. 'What's this we hear about Steve? Is it true?' she asked.

'It's true; unfortunately it is true,' I muttered.

'*Modimo!* (God!) These people are at war. Black people must wake up. We can't sit back and do nothing.'

It was a simple, direct cry from the heart and all I said was that she was right.

'*Modimo,* Steve. *Bathong!* (O, people!)' she exclaimed once again, her voice choking.

I telephoned several other people. A minister of religion said he was disgusted and said something about the need for a judicial inquiry. A coloured woman broke down and wept. Black South Africa was devastated. It was a loss they couldn't handle. There was anger and bitterness and a feeling of helplessness all round. Some knew Steve personally, some had only heard of or read about him; yet they all acknowledged and respected his leadership.

Jimmy Kruger, the Minister of Justice, had simply announced that Biko died in detention after a hunger strike. For a week, according to the Minister, he had refused his food rations. But Biko was, as Motlana put it, a healthy robust young man to die of starvation after a week's hunger strike.

I first learnt about Biko and his Black Consciousness ideas when I read a news report from, I think, the *Sunday Times* early in 1971 or thereabout. He had addressed a conference of national black and white student organisations, including those from the Afrikaanse Studentebond, in Cape Town. His exposition of the then South African political situation was off the beaten track; it was completely fresh, brilliant and breath-taking. Whereas before the banning of African political organisations after Sharpeville in 1960, African leaders had generally sought collaboration with progressive liberal whites in the struggle for a place in the sun, the young black students, as reflected in the utterance of Steve Biko, were charting a totally different route. They believed that association with whites emasculated the struggle for liberation, rendering it ineffective, if not utterly meaningless and wanted to go it alone. They claimed whites had, through their racist, oppressive policies, defined themselves as part of the problem that they, as black people, faced and could therefore, never be part of its solution. The biggest mistake blacks made, Biko asserted, was to assume that every white who opposed apartheid was an ally.

In Biko's own words:

A new breed of black leaders was beginning to take a dim view of the involvement of (white) liberals in a struggle that they regarded as essentially theirs, when the political movements of the blacks were either banned or harassed into non-existence. This left the stage open once more for the liberals to continue with their work of fighting for the rights of blacks. It never occurred to the liberals that the integration they insisted upon as an effective way of opposing apartheid was impossible to achieve in South Africa. It had to be artificial because it was being foistered on two parties whose entire upbringing had been to support the lie that one race was superior and others inferior. One has to overhaul the whole system in South Africa before hoping to see black and white walking hand in hand to oppose a common enemy. As it is, black and white walk into a hastily organised integrated circle carrying with them the seeds of destruction of that circle – their inferiority and superiority complexes.

The myth of integration as propounded under the banner of liberal ideology must be cracked and killed because it makes people believe that something is being done when in reality the artificially integrated circles are a soporific to the blacks while salving the consciences of guilt-stricken whites. It works from the false premise that because it is difficult to bring people from different races together in this country, achievement of this in itself a step towards the total liberation of blacks. Nothing could be more misleading.

[*Protest to challenge,* Vol. 5, 1964-1979, Thomas G Karis and Gail M Gerhart]

Not long after reading this *Sunday Times* report, I met Harry Nengwekhulu, a student leader who, it turned out, worked with Biko in rallying together studends at black university campuses, urging them to join the nascent exclusive black South African

Student Organisation (Saso). Nengwekhulu had come from Turfloop in Pietersburg (now Polokwane) to Johannesburg where I worked as a reporter for *The Star* newspaper. And, like all Africans who came from such rural areas to the towns and cities, he was experiencing difficulties because of influx control laws, which forbade entry there without official authorisation or permit. It was as a result of this chance meeting, I think, that I eventually met Biko who, at about that time was a regular visitor at Turfloop (University of the North), where he was campaigning for Saso membership. It also turned out the student organisation had just established an office in Jorissen Street, Braamfontein, hardly fifteen minutes walk from the place of my employment at 47 Sauer Street.

Although I don't quite recall precisely my first encounter with Biko, I often listened and spoke to him at conferences, usually at St Peter's Seminary in Hammanskraal, north of Pretoria (now Tshwane) and at smaller assemblies arranged in private homes in the townships. I saw the tall, athletic and broad-faced founder president of Saso at work. I had even worked side by side with Biko in a commission appointed by Saso and BPC in 1972 to look into the possibility of establishing a black press. Although I was a member neither of Saso nor of BPC, I had been asked to give a helping hand. And it was during such moments that I came to know him pretty well.

In a sense, Biko was Black Consciousness (BC). He had, as it were, appropriated the concept. He had realised that his people were immensely fearful, fearful of whites; that it was this fear and feeling of inferiority that not only made them despise themselves, but also quiver and grovel in the presence of whites. Black Conciousness demanded of black people to shed that fear, the feeling of inferiority, the poor self-esteem; to take pride in being what they are and to appreciate their own culture, tradition and history; to jettison the habit of seeing themselves through the eyes of their oppressors; to develop a new outlook in which they would see themselves through their own eyes.

Black Consciousness denounced, for instance, giving black children white names, as a reflection of self-hate. So was hair straightening and the use of skin lightening lotions or creams, which it saw as a desire to 'look white'. The term 'non-white', commonly used by whites when referring to people of colour, was also considered highly derogatory and, therefore, unacceptable. 'We are black. We want everybody, including whites, to refer to us a such,' Biko and his lieutenants insisted, explaining that the term 'black' referred to the oppressed within with the country: African, coloured and Indian peoples. Black, they preached, was not only beautiful, but black people were in fact on their own, alone in the quest for freedom. Indeed, blackness had become the rallying cry for unity and solidarity in the struggle for liberation. Needless to say, the new philosophy was inculcating – with deliberate intent – a spirit of self-love, self-reliance, self-confidence and self-assertiveness, as well as rejection of the notion that people of colour were an inferior species. Biko was, or so it seemed, the heart and soul of this revolution. He was a good listener and a good talker, richly endowed with ideas and the ability to communicate them to other people. A return to master may help us better understand and appreciate the then prevailing black student intellectualism.

Biko argued:

> *The emergence of Saso and its tough policy of non-involvement with the white world set people's minds thinking along new lines. This was a challenge to the age-old tradition in South Africa that opposition to apartheid was enough to qualify whites for acceptance by the black world. Despite protest and charges of racialism from liberal-minded white students, the black students stood firm in their rejection of the principle of unholy alliances between blacks and whites…*

> *The call for Black Consciousness is the most positive call to come from any group in the black world for a long time. It is more than just a reactionary rejection of whites by blacks. The quintessence of it is the realisation by blacks that, in order to feature well in this game of power politics, they have to use the concept of group power and to build a strong foundation for this. Being an historically, socially and economically disinherited and disposed group, they have the strongest foundation from which to operate. The philosophy of Black Consciousness, therefore, expresses group pride and the determination by the blacks to rise and attain the envisaged self. At the heart of this kind of thinking is the realisation by the blacks that the most potent weapon in the hands of the oppressor is the mind of the oppressed. Once the latter has been so effectively manipulated and controlled by the oppressor as to make the oppressed believe that he is a liability to the white man, then there will be nothing the oppressed can do that will scare the powerful masters. Hence thinking along lines of Black Consciousness makes the black man see himself as a being, entire in himself, and not as an extension of a broom or lever to some machine. At the end of it all, he cannot tolerate attempts by anybody to dwarf the significance of his manhood...*

[*Protest to Challenge,* Vol. 5, 1964-1979, Thomas G Karis & Gail M Gerhart]

Admittedly, Biko was neither a saint nor a sinner. He had his strengths and weaknesses. He loved life, black and white. He was mature enough to acknowledge that not all that was black was good nor all that was white bad; that there were good black and white people just as there were bad black and white people. It was, therefore, the oppressive system – not the people administering it – that he hated and sought to eliminate. He sought, too, to create in the minds of his people an appropriate image of themselves. For he knew that the major stumbling block among them was self-hate (when you're despised virtually all round, you begin in the long run to believe that you are indeed worthless), and thus the keen desire to run away from themselves, from reality, to become what they were not. He set out to correct that disastrous mental attitude, so that the people could begin to see themselves through their own eyes. He sought to enthuse them with a spirit of self-love. To enable them to develop pride in what they really were. He was aware too that standing in the way was not only an inferiority complex, but also the divisions promoted by the system. He often called upon the people to realise that only through unity could they attain their goals. And, because he believed whites were responsible for turning blacks into the creatures they were, he saw no role for whites to play in the battle to overcome their problems. Only when blacks had attained the desired self-pride could they and whites think of working together. For then they would be meeting as equals, no longer as master and servant.

A hard-working visionary, Biko was also extremely persuasive. Emotional talk was not his beat. Whenever he spoke, he appealed to people's minds, not their emotions. He discouraged arrogance among BC supporters and stressed the importance of involvement in relevant organisation in their communities. The movement had to establish and run community projects to gain support. Deeds were, after all, more eloquent than words.

Biko always seemed busiest at the conferences, privately planning and formulating whatever programmes he reckoned had to be considered for adoption. However, Biko, a jolly and fun-loving chap who mixed freely with people, any people, still found time to relax. At the end of each day he retreated, usually in the company of friends, to some room to relax, often sipping beer. He would listen to other people, laugh and talk whenever he had to. And it would not be until the small hours of the morning that he would go to bed.

The Black Press Commission was created in an atmosphere of unrealism. Many Saso and BPC activists seemed not to have the foggiest idea about the running of a newspaper. They denounced advertising and claimed that the kind of journal they envisaged would have to do without adverts. Adverts, they said, encouraged blacks, especially women, to try to look like whites. Of course, they were reacting to the cult of wigs, hair straightening and skin-lightening, and I feared the mood would cripple their laudable efforts. Where would the proposed journal get its revenue if advertising was ruled out? Did the organisation have a multi-millionaire behind their project? Even if they had, how long would he be prepared to sink his millions into such an unbusiness-like venture?

I was reluctant to associate myself with a scheme that was so patently unrealistic. So I expressed fears to Biko. What sort of newspaper did they have in mind? Who was backing them financially? And how long would he be prepared to back them in a venture without returns? Didn't he know advertising was the life blood of any newspaper? He believed, he said, a national newspaper, perhaps a monthly to begin with, was ideal. The main thing was what policy it would have. He was convinced that the journal would be supported if it embraced the principles of Black Consciousness in its policy. He was not worried by the hostile attitude towards adverts because he considered it a minor problem that could be overcome with ease. All the commission would need to do would be to stress the importance of advertising only after everything had been formulated. If the apparent opposition was convinced there could be a newspaper without advertising, it would fizzle out. There was no financial backer and he felt the greatest problem for the commission would be to determine what means and ways it could recommend for fund-raising. On the basis of those funds the project would stand or fall. He himself believed the money had to come from the black people themselves, because only that way were they likely to accept it as being really their own newspaper.

At the first sitting inside the Saso office in Beatrice Street, Durban, the commission did not go into its work in any depth. Members merely spent the day laying the groundwork for future activities. Biko, in the company of some close friends, took me to dinner at a restaurant somewhere near the coast. Thereafter, we went to an evening show where we remained until about 10pm. Then we moved out to Strini Moodley's flat in another part of the town. We were to spend the rest of the evening there with some friends. It turned out to be a drinking session, interspersed with spirited political talk and a sporadic dancing to jazz music from a record player. The night dragged on wearily, but my host remained alert, energetic until daybreak. Then he said we should go home to catch some sleep as there was some meeting he wanted to attend later that morning. He took me to his home at Umlazi, I think, where I dropped into bed. He woke me up barely three hours later.

'Food is ready; we should not miss the meeting,' he said. He had already washed!

'Do I have to go to the meeting too?' I moaned.

'Why not. Are you being lazy?'

'I am not yet rested.'

'Come on, there's no time for sleep; haven't you heard the land was stolen from us while we slept,' he laughed.

'Well, I suppose I have no choice.'

He laughed again, going away; then he returned with warm water for washing. I was feeling miserable and really wished that he would leave me alone to sleep. Eventually I pulled myself together and got ready.

We had our meal in the sitting room and it was while we were eating that I learnt the meeting he felt he had to attend had nothing to do with Saso. Some local residents wanted to tackle some problems in the community. He had made up his mind to attend, and so identify with the people. Several men kept coming in and out. They all knew him and seemed to come in merely to greet him. He introduced me only to some. He never mentioned the meeting to any of them. It was the beginning of a long hard day.

Accompanied by Barney Pityana, then Saso secretary-general, and Bokwe Mafuna, BCP field worker, we went to the meeting at a local school. Only men were in attendance. I didn't know whether women were barred, and I did not discuss their absence with anybody. Mafuna, Pityana and Biko all participated in the meeting with vitality and, at the end of the deliberations Biko and Pityana were among the people elected into the executive committee. The meeting dispersed at about sunset. I thought then that we were returning home. But no, we drove to another part of the township. Biko and his colleagues wanted to see some Anglican pastor. They wanted him to allow them to run literacy classes in his church hall. We found the pastor home at the parish. Later that evening I learnt from Biko that the deal had been clinched.

It was Biko in action, living up to his ideals. At first he had involved himself in Nusas, the white-dominated National Union of South African Students. Disenchanted with working with whites, he attended a meeting of the University Christian Movement in 1967. He and others led a walk-out of black students. They rejected the multi-racial organisation and formed the exclusively black Saso the following year, with Biko himself as its first president. Because of insistence that Saso remain exclusively black, his detractors considered him a racist. Conveniently, they overlooked his expressed belief that Black Consciousness was meant for blacks to liberate themselves psychologically. He and his executive travelled the country extensively seeking support. The going was tough, but they won the battle against Nusas for the black students' vote.

Essentially Saso was an organisation for students. But its mission, as reflected in the utterances and activities of Biko and his lieutenants, was much bigger. It went beyond student politics. The leadership went out of its way to exert its influence in all aspects of black South African life whether it be cultural, labour-related, religious or political. But how well organised was Saso and how widespread its BC gospel? There was no way of knowing, of measuring its strength. The media was not only giving it scant attention, but continued insulting the students by referring to them as 'non-whites' despite their objection. However, the students continued resolutely and relentlessly campaigning within their communities.

The leadership, which included reporter Bokwe Mafuna of the now defunct *Rand Daily Mail* newspaper, played some part in the formation, for instance, of the Union of Black Journalists, with me as its first president, in 1971. In the same year the Black People's Convention (BPC), a Black Consciousness outfit, was mooted (thanks to Harry Nengwekhulu) and eventually inaugurated early in 1972, specifically to address black political aspirations. (Tom Moerane, president of the Association for Educational and Cultural Advancement of Africans and editor of *The World* newspaper, had convened a conference in December 1971 at the DOCC in Orlando East, Soweto. In his opening remarks, he said they gathered there to form an umbrella body under which existing organisations would operate. Harry Nengwekhulu rose to object, saying black people wanted a national organisation to address their political aspirations and not more cultural bodies that did nothing for them. An argument ensued. Moerane was forced to put the matter to a vote. Nengwekhulu won the vote and took the meeting. An ad hoc committee was formed to pursue further the issue of establishing a national political body. In consequence, BPC was established in 1972.)

Some people may argue that it was mere coincidence that individuals such as Mongane Wally Serote and Oswald Mtshali seriously began writing and publishing poetry, expressing their inner feelings and interpreting their experiences, during the 1970s. In my opinion, this new generation of poets was the result of the vigorous teachings of Black Consciousness, encouraging blacks confidently to communicate their experiences. Another notable feature of the era was the rise in the field of arts and entertainment, of drama and theatre groups such as the Soweto Black Ensemble, Mihlothi Black Theatre (both of them in Johannesburg), the Serpent Players (Port Elizabeth) and the Theatre Council of Natal (Durban). Besides, a Black Workers Council was founded ostensibly to conscientise and co-ordinate black workers regarding the importance of unity and solidarity, as well as their role in black development. A definite new sense of pride and self-rediscovery had indeed emerged with people recording and depicting their feelings and experiences. Talking about his own development as a writer, Mongane Serote says:

> *I kept close contact with other writers formally and informally. We wrote letters to each other: Mafika Pascal Gwala, James Matthews, Richard Rive, Sipho Sepamla and Oswald Mtshali, etc. This was the time of the emergence of the Black Consciousness Movement. The BC propounders were an extreme threat to the white public who to a very large extent owned the means of exposure for writers. Newspapers, magazines and publishers would ask whether you were a BC poet or not. If you were, you tended to be labeled a racist.*

[Interview with Jaki Seroke, *Staffrider,* April/May 1981]

However, it was not until May 1972 that the country was rudely awakened to the overwhelming power of black students. Authorities at Turfloop (the University of the North) had, in reaction to a student class boycott which was precipitated by the expulsion of Abram Onkgopotse Tiro, closed the institution. Students on other black campuses – Fort Hare, University of the Zululand, Western Cape and Wentworth (black section of University of Natal) – immediately boycotted classes in solidarity with their counterparts at Turfloop.

The expulsion of Tiro from Turfloop crippled black tertiary education countrywide. Suddenly, Saso became newsworthy. My news editor asked me to keep tabs on the student organisation daily to find out what was happening.

Barely three months later, the South African media was forced by the students to drop the use of the term 'non-white'. The evening before the student congress was to start at St Peter's Seminary, the leaders announced to media representatives that any newspaper that referred to them as 'non-whites' would be thrown out forthwith. Lo and behold, the liberal morning daily, *The Rand Daily Mail,* was apparently not listening. It disregarded the announcement. The students were furious. Before congress commenced we sat quietly at the elevated press table as delegate after delegate attacked us for 'arrogantly disregarding' their appeal not to insult them and demanded our immediate expulsion.

However, Steve Biko saved the day for some of us. He was forthright. 'Comrades', he said, 'we are gathered here to deliberate on issues that affect our people. They need to know the decisions we take at this congress. It will be unwise to expel all newspapers when only one of them has insulted us.' In consequence, only representatives of *The Rand Daily Mail* were ordered to leave. Tony Holiday, a white reporter, rose to leave and as he went out his black colleague, Bokwe Mafune, stood up to announce his immediate resignation as reporter for the newspaper. There was deafening applause as he stepped down into the hall, joining the delegates. And the term non-white was never used again, even by Afrikaans-language newspapers. Needless to say, though, the offending word has intermittently been creeping back into use following the post-1994 political dispensation.

Biko's other obsession was the establishment of an exclusively black national newspaper and a publishing house. He set about achieving this in a number of ways, including the five-member Black Press Commission that was formed under his leadership in October 1972, to look into the feasibility of putting up such ventures. He had, possibly through his column, *I Write What I Like,* also consolidated the Saso *Newsletter,* the student organisation's mouthpiece, into a respectable opinion–maker. Furthermore, he was instrumental in the formation of the Black Community Programmes, a project co–ordinating body that was responsible for the publication, for instance, of *Creativity and Development,* a collection of papers delivered at Saso conferences, as well as *Black Review,* an annual review of black activities and projects. The Black Press Commission comprised Howard Lawrence, Ben Langa, Bokwe Mafuna, Lenamile (his first name escapes me) and me. It was expected to report back by early 1973. That it never reported was not due to any incompetence or lack of trying on the part of the commissioners. Several meetings were held. However, these efforts were overtaken by events when eight BC leaders, including Biko, Barney Pityana, Harry Nengwekhulu and Bokwe Mafuna were banned in March 1973 for a period of five years. As a result of the banning, Biko was forced to leave Durban for his home town in the Eastern Cape, where he was restricted to the magisterial district of King William's Town. He could, as a result, neither write for publications nor speak in public.

Steve Biko was born of ordinary black parents in Ginsberg, King William's Town in the Eastern Cape on 18 December 1946. He received his primary education locally but went to Marianhill, a Roman Catholic institution in Natal, for his secondary school education. He matriculated in 1965 and entered the University of Natal black section (Wentworth) in 1966 to study medicine. It was while he was a medical student at Wentworth that he became involved in student politics, first with the multiracial Nusas, and two years later, when he broke away from Nusas, with the exclusively black Saso, becoming its first president, and adopting the Black Consciousness philosophy as the organisation's abiding ideological standpoint. Apparently as he involved himself deeper and deeper in politics, Biko's studies suffered, to the extent that he was expelled from Wentworth, allegedly because of poor academic performance, in 1972. Thereafter he decided, it seems, to devote himself full-time to BC activities and began working for the Black Community Programmes (BCP) in Durban. The BCP had been established to enable black people to appreciate their identity; to create a sense of their own power; to develop a black leadership capable of guiding the development of their communities; to get their own communities to organise themselves and analyse their needs, as well as problems, and to mobilise resources in order to meet those needs.

Still very aware of the importance of education, and undaunted by his expulsion from Wentworth, Biko enrolled with the University of South Africa (Unisa) as a part-time student to do a junior degree in law, while serving the five-year banning order. It is noteworthy that during this period of his confinement, Biko did not only build BCP into a respected organisation in King William's Town, but also established the Zanempilo Health Clinic in 1974 as part of the wider and more general BCP project aimed at providing essential services – curative and preventative – that were lacking in adjacent rural communities.

According to Charles Nqakula, author and journalist who is now the minister of Safety and Security, St Chad's Anglican Church at 15 Leopold Street, King William's Town, where the Saso office was based, was the heartbeat of all BC activities in the town, if not the whole of the Eastern Cape, after Steve Biko was banished and restricted there in 1973. 'Fifteen Leopold Street', Ngakula states, 'was once the epitome of the black liberation struggle as was interpreted by the Black Consciousness Movement. It was from there [that] the Zanempilo project and others were initiated and the centre also served as headquarters for BCP publications – *Black Viewpoint* and *Black Review*.' [Umhlaba Wethu: Historical Indictment, Editor Mothobi Mutloatse, Skotaville 1989]

Mafika Pascal Gwala has said:

> *Steve proved he wasn't the has-been who would sit back*
> *and rest on counting the A's he'd scored at school or tally the*

> *glories of his early days as Saso leader. Against all the lies*
> *and provocations levelled at black organisations – against the*
> *ANC, PAC, BPC and student groups such as Saso, Sasm,*
> *NAYO – Steve's BPC branch saw to it that every story was*
> *investigated, the findings scrutinised and compiled into a*
> *BCP publication. Thus many a hitherto unrevealed truth or*
> *factor was brought out before the blacks, as part of their*
> *experience within the apartheid society.*

[*Reconstruction*: *90 Years of Black Historical Literature*, Compiler &
Editor Mothobi Mutloatse, Ravan Press, 1981]

The restrictive banning order confining Biko to King
William's Town turned out to be the beginning of continuous
police harassment. He was charged with breaking the banning
order the following year. His crime? He had written a Unisa
examination in a crowded hall and so mixed with other people –
in contravention of the banning order. In April 1976 the security
police summoned him for allegedly crossing the road at a stop
street. He appeared in court in his own defence and was
acquitted. After the outbreak of the 1976 Soweto student
uprising, he was detained and spent more than 100 days in solitary
confinement. Not long after his release, he was arrested and
charged with attempting to defeat the ends of justice. The police
claimed that he had persuaded witnesses – in a case arising from
the student unrest – to testify that the statements they made to the
police were made under duress. He was, however, acquitted on
Wednesday, 13 June 1977. In the face of all this, why didn't Biko
escape to campaign in exile? He believed he couldn't do much
operating in exile. For him, the battle was here at home and he
felt very strongly, that he had to be around even though he only
worked from behind the scenes. That was the nature of the man:
courageous, selfless and highly committed to the service of his
people.

It has been claimed that at the time of his last arrest, Biko was returning from Cape Town where he had been trying to unite the exiled black liberation movements. This is plausible, because division not only between the exiled liberation organisations, but also among the oppressed black masses within the country, was his greatest concern. Just as he had – through the concept of BC – been battling to bring together Africans, coloureds and Indians in the quest for a better tomorrow, he now wanted to unite the exiled liberation movements in order to maximise the crucial Black Power needed to bring down the apartheid edifice.

Biko died at the hands of the security police barely a month after he was detained in August. The shameless arrogance with which his death was explained away (the so-called Minister of Justice Jimmy Kruger actually stated publicly that the death left him cold); the unending detentions, bannings and banishment, as well as the subsequent banning on Wednesday, 19 October 1977 of virtually all BC organisations (BPC, Saso, BCP, Sasm, Black Women's Federations and UBJ among them), *The World* and *Weekend World* newspapers and the multi-racial Christian Institute; the outright rejection of both the Black Parents Association (BPA) and the Committee of Ten, plus the take-over by government of some schools, showed convincingly that the callous white rulers had hardened their bigoted attitudes towards *people of colour* in general and in particular the African people. In their view, black demands were shrouded in Communism and had to been crushed at all cost. BPA and the Committee of Ten had been rejected despite overwhelming public support. The government still preferred to deal only with its own men and women, people who would serve its interests and not those of the community.

There was nothing new in that kind of attitude really. The history of the black man was scarred with similar denials. Even in the so-called homelands the dice were heavily loaded against the people. This was part of the grand design, the divide–and–rule tactic. The people of Soweto had destroyed the UBC, a statutory structure, and denounced administration boards. For that they could not be forgiven. But the young were just as adamant. Their demands had grown. No longer were they fighting the Afrikaans issue, it was now the whole system of oppression. They wanted freedom, social, political and economic freedom; they demanded the land. '*Si khalela izwe lethu,*' they sang stridently as they buried their dead. After the youth had paralysed education in the townships by forcing the teachers to resign, the government took control of post-primary schools. However, they refused to register for enrolment. Their influence had become too strong, awesomely strong. No adult organisation could prosper without their recognition and support. And they seemed ready at every turn to produce new leaders, replacing those either taken into police custody or those forced to run away from the country.

Above all they were still in the street, as defiant as ever.

In its desire to crush the unrest, government sought the support of the media. Jimmy Kruger believed, wrongly, that *The World* was inciting the people, that it was promoting hostility between the races. Now *The World* was Percy Qoboza and Percy Qoboza was *The World*. The two had done and were doing immeasureable harm. All would be fine, if Qoboza could be stopped from following that disastrous course. Simply, Kruger wanted the newspaper to abandon its job: telling the black community what was happening, that the cause of their bitterness, frustration and tension was none other than the government itself.

Suddenly editor Qoboza became the target. He and his family were threatened with death. A bomb exploded in front of his home. It shattered windows on the morning of 19 September, a week after Biko's death. It had been thrown at the house from the street. Nobody was injured, but some articles were damaged. Qoboza belonged to no political organisation. Although he had been instrumental in the formation of the Committee of Ten, he was neither a member nor had he attended any of the committee meetings. So he was being attacked, we must presume, by agents of people who found his newspaper's coverage of events in the townships intolerable.

Then came Wednesday, 19 October 1977 when once again the security police stirred, going into action long before dawn. In Soweto, they collected members of the Committee of Ten. Motlana was bundled out of his home soon after 4am. So were Kraai, Mathabathe, Kuzwayo, Ramokgopa, Mazibuko, Mayathula, Manthata, Mosala and Lolwane. Several others, among them Hlaku Rachidi, BPC's national president, and Aubrey Mokoena, were raided and hauled in. Still others found police waiting for them when they arrived at work later that morning. They were detained, too. *The World* and eighteen organisations, including the SSRC, BPA, BPC, Saso, BCP, the black Women's Federation, Sasm, UBJ and the multi-racial Christian Institute were banned.

Altogether about sixty people were detained countrywide. Some were detained under the Terrorism Act, but most under the Internal Security Act. Virtually all black opposition to apartheid had been immobilised, many families deprived of breadwinners and thousands more left stranded with the banning of the BCP. Then the cops came for Qoboza, as he was still trying to hold a press conference to explain to the world what had happened to his newspapers – *The World* and *Weekend World*. He too was roped in. The organisations and publications had been banned because, in the eyes of the government, they endangered maintenance of public order. Kruger assured the nation that this was based on facts gathered by eminent citizens during secret investigations. It was a shocking revelation. These people and organisations had been subjected to probing, secret inquiry. Evidence had been gathered against them, judgment based on that evidence made and punishment meted out. But they didn't know. They had no idea what evidence had been collected, where it came from, or who the judges were. A chilling state of affairs.

It was the end of an era, the era of open black political expression. What the future held in store, no one could tell for sure. We could only speculate. In 1960 when the ANC and the PAC were banned, the two organisations had immediately gone underground whence they adopted violence as a means to bring about change. Chances for such a feeling were even greater in 1977 than they had been seventeen years before, and it seemed the next uprising would be bloodier than anything experienced since 16 June 1976.

CHAPTER 13

LESSON TO THE LEARNED

Mayhem, murder, terrorism virtually everywhere: inside congested passenger trains, at railway stations and bus and taxi ranks teeming with commuters. A decade when vigilantes and hit squads, as well as their minions – the hostel-dwellers, nonchalantly brutalised township residents at home, in the streets and in moving trains; when political activists used the hideous 'necklace' (a petrol-soaked tyre set alight around the neck of a victim, usually a suspected or alleged police informer) as murder weapon; the second phase of black student revolt against racist white rule. Yes, those were the 1980s, bloodier than anything seen before in South Africa.

As we approached the volatile period, two contestants – the Congress of South African Students (Cosas) and the Azanian Student Organisation (Azaso) – were the main political forces among the country's embattled black youth. Established in June and November 1979 respectively, Cosas, which at its inception adopted the Freedom Charter as is guiding spirit, represented pre-university students while Azaso, an offspring of the philosophy of Black Consciousness, represented students at university level. Despite their ideological differences and approaches, both student bodies seemed set and determined for the big shove (or was it a shake-up?) of the apartheid juggernaut. Also, we already had the Azanian People's Organisation (Azapo), the leading torch-bearer of Black Consciousness that had risen out of the ashes of the Black People's Convention, on the political landscape.

However, as fate would have it, the BC forces were crippled at the outset. Azapo suspended Curtis Nkondo, its president, in January 1980 for breach of principle. (Nkondo had, among other things, appealed to white politician Helen Suzman to negotiate with the government on his behalf for the release of a detained brother.) But in suspending its president, Azapo alienated its student wing. When Azaso's demand that Nkondo be reinstated as president was ignored, Azaso vowed to co-operate fully with Cosas in the struggle for liberation.

Thus it was really the invigorated Cosas that now strode the length and breadth of the country exhorting, not only students (black and white), but black teachers and parents as well, to join hands in the battle for a brighter future. In a call to parents, teachers and students to attend a meeting in March 1980, the Charterist student body laid down student grievances: there was a general shortage of textbooks and the books that were available were too expensive for parents to afford; the number of teachers was in adequate, with some not being paid; students were being brutalised, with girls physically assaulted in certain instances; students were being forced to buy stationery and to pay 'voluntary' fees, they were forbidden to establish SRCs (Student Representative Councils); the wearing of uniforms was strictly enforced and uniforms were too expensive; students were also being evicted from classrooms because they could not cope with the school work and they were forced to do subjects they would not need in their future careers. Although there was a boom and an increase in the price of gold, Cosas went on, commerce and industry needed cheap labour. The organisation ended its list of grievances with a plea to parents to rise and protect students because the future of their children was at stake.

There were lessons, Cosas acknowledged, to be learnt from the June 1976 uprising. It had learnt that students were a special grouping in that, unlike parents, they had few constraints in involving themselves in political activity, and had begun questioning their future roles in society. It had also been realised that protest in the form of spontaneous confrontation with the state could not be effective: new strategies and organisational approaches had to be developed. The 1976 uprising, Cosas believed, had instilled in the youth an increased political consciousness as well.

However, student action was limited in what it could achieve and, as such, the objectives of students had to be realistically and tactically defined. No matter how militant, 'student action was not likely to be capable of overthrowing the system of oppression and exploitation known as apartheid. It was precisely that system that lay at the centre of student grievances. Our resistance is a response to spaces the capitalism system wanted us to fill,' said the student organisation in its Number 1 quarterly journal, *Cosas National Newsletter* of March/April 1983.

In addition to mobilising public meetings, pamphleteering and issuing T-shirts, Cosas organised funerals of students fatally shot by police during marches and protest campaigns, commemorated 16 June and the brutal death of Steve Biko at the hands of police. They also held services mourning the execution of Solomon Mahlangu.

With the slogan *Each One Teach One,* Cosas held its 1982 national congress in Cape Town in May and adopted *Student Worker Action* as the theme with which to educate its members about the workers' struggle and how it was related to that of students. The decisions they took included holding quarterly national councils where the development and growth of branches would be reviewed. Branch activities would also be assessed at such meetings before any further action could be taken.

Students, it was hoped, would educate each other through the slogan *Each One Teach One*, about the prevailing political situation and so become involved in the organisation's structures, making it possible for them to be part of the struggle for liberation. Also, the organisation's newsletter would be used to spread its message: striving for a dynamic, free and compulsory education for all; creating a spirit of trust and co-operation between students, parents and teachers; and informing one another about how to form SRC structures in order to sustain their activities.

Members were urged to contribute articles to the newsletter. The first newsletter carried stories, among others, on multiracial sport, detentions and bannings, while the second (October/November 1983) ran articles on past school boycotts, showed the picture of Hector Pieterson, the first victim of the 1976 uprising, and printed samples of how to apply for a bursary.

At its fourth national council, held at Wentworth, Durban, in December 1982 and attended by regional representatives from all over the country except the Eastern Cape delegation it was pointed out that lack of finances was the big problem hampering growth. (The Eastern Cape delegation, council learnt, was detained by Transkei police while on its way to the meeting.) It was said too that Eastern and Western Cape regions had established regional councils. The meeting immediately adopted as policy of the organisation the establishment of regional councils that were expected to review all activities of members at school level and the responses of students, parents and teachers to such activities, as well as to determine membership in each branch. Council was informed that there were thus far forty-four branches countrywide. Regions were urged to go all out in organising and establishing more branches to make their next national council in June 1983 a success.

And as they buried the dead and commemorated historic events, Cosas members and their supporters chanted slogans galore and freedom songs, among them, *Forward we go / Backward never / Aluta continua / Amandla ngawethu / Matla ke a rona / Student of SA unite / And fight Bantu Education.* 'Long live the struggle,' they went; 'one for all and all for one; unity is strength', they chanted intermittently. They were emboldened by the realisation that the movement was indeed growing, despite police harassment. Cosas was convinced its repeated calls for workers (parents and teachers) to come to the revolutionary party had at long last been heeded when in January 1983 a steering committee was set up to establish the United Democratic Front (UDF), following a call by Dr Allan Boesak, president of the World Alliance of Reformed Churches. That resistance against apartheid was gaining momentum was no longer in doubt, perhaps even to the government as it went about formulating its more divisive new constitutional plans aimed, among other things, at creating black local authorities and removing black people from so-called 'black spots' for resettlement in the Bantustans (homelands). (The UDF was launched nationally in August when 1 000 delegates, representing some 575 organisations, met at Mitchells Plain in Cape Town. The delegates had come from trade unions, civic and sporting organisations, women and youth bodies.)

Cosas rejected the country's education system as rendering black people perpetual slaves, maintaining white supremacy and dividing the people into ethnic enclaves. According to its policy document it sought the kind of education that would enable people to think and act freely and envisaged a society where free and compulsory education would no longer be a privilege, but rather a right; a society where citizens would be taught to love one another and to maintain their culture and dignity as well as to honour human brotherhood. As an anti-racial body, Cosas rejected the 'present system of multiracial sport as an attempt by the government to create an impression of genuine change so as to gain international recognition' and would only recognise non-racial sport from grassroots level. The kind of religion introduced by the colonialists 'with the aim of keeping the oppressed inferior and subservient to the oppressor,' was also rejected, while being recognised as a living reality and being identified with the social problems of the oppressed. The government strategy of 'granting concessions to a sector of our society as an attempt to create a middle class in order to render the struggle ineffective' was unacceptable too.

In December 1982 after a joint session of Cosas and Azaso, it was announced that a major campaign for 1983 would aim at helping students to develop a greater understanding of education. However, 1983 turned out to be the most difficult year. Several members of Cosas were arrested in connection with a petrol bomb attack on the house of Ciskei's deputy minister of defence. By the end of September more than half of the East London branch and almost the entire executive in Zwelitsha were in detention. All schools but one – Mzomhle High School – in Mdantsane were empty with both teachers and students staying away. When the Ciskeian authorities withheld salaries of teachers of those schools affected by the class boycotts, teachers at Mzomhle High School returned their salaries in protest and solidarity with the affected teachers. Other areas affected by the school boycotts included Duncan Village, Litha, Sada and Zwelitsha. The Detainees Parents Support Group in East London said that when students rejected orders to return to school, they became target for vigilantes. The vigilantes, it was claimed, went from house to house taking children to isolated spots and beating them with sjamboks and sticks. Children of school-going age seen in the streets were also apprehended. Furthermore, people released from detention claimed the security police believed Cosas was a front for the banned African National Congress. Whether or not this was because the student organisation had earlier in 1983 commemorated various historical events in which the ANC had participated, events such as the twenty-eighth anniversary of Freedom Charter and the 1956 women's march to Union Buildings in Pretoria protesting against passes, we could not tell for sure. We could only speculate.

In 1983 student activities, especially in the Transvaal, entailed protests over the age-limit for students to remain at school, rent increases, the demolition of shack settlements and bus boycotts, according to Cosas, which also reported that several activists in the

Eastern Cape, including student leaders Siphiwe Mtimkhulu and Topsy Mdaka, were missing. Almost always those missing were presumed to have been either detained by the security police or murdered by vigilantes, if not by the specially-trained hit squads.

As we entered 1984, Cosas adopted *United Action for Democratic Education* as it's theme for the year, proclaiming that the theme would be its main issue in what it called the Education Charter Campaign. The idea of an Education Charter Campaign was first mooted at an Azaso Congress in 1982. 'The events of June 1976, the boycotts of 1980, the protest of 1981, have all centred,' Cosas explained, 'around the need for an alternative education. Democratic education reflects the needs of our people. It is their needs which should be primary in society at large and in education in particular.'

However, 1984 was barely a month old when widespread disturbances began, shortly after schools reopened in January. By the beginning of April, some 13 107 primary-school children at twenty-four schools in Atteridgeville (Pretoria), the Eastern Cape, Soweto, and Alexandra were boycotting classes. Initially, their grievances were educational, but by the middle of the year pupils joined community organisations and workers protesting against the government's July increase from seven to ten per cent in general sales tax (GST), the coloured and Indian general elections for the new Tricameral Parliament in August, and rises in township rent service charges. Protests during the Tricameral Elections led, particularly in the case of the Indian election, to violence. On the day of the coloured election, 800 000 pupils and students boycotted classes, with coloured pupils alone accounting for 630 000 of the total. [Race Relation Survey 1984, SAIRR, Johannesburg]

Once again violence flared on 3 September during a one-day stay-away in the Vaal Triangle townships when residents protested against proposed monthly service charge increases of R5, 90 for state-owned houses and R5, 50 for privately-owned houses. Sixty per cent of workers and almost all of the 93 000 pupils in the area stayed away. A three-year-old white boy, Blair Gordon, was stoned to death by a crowd of youth attending a funeral on 12 September. Cosas' Soweto branch secretary Bongani Kumalo was allegedly shot dead by police the day before. Thirty-one other people were reported to have been killed, among them community councillors. The Release Mandela Committee (RMC), an affiliate of the UDF, called for another one-day stay-away on 17 September in Soweto, in solidarity with people in the Vaal Triangle and in protest against police action in the townships. Although the RMC intended the boycott to last only one day, it ended in confusion and violence when some residents stayed away for two days and others resisted it altogether. Estimates of the numbers who stayed away ranged between thirty-five and sixty-five per cent. A third stay-away, in Kwa Thema on the East Rand on 22 October, was organised by the KwaThema Parent/Student Committee to express solidarity with boycotting pupils. Over eighty per cent of workers in the area stayed away from work. Estimates were that between 300 000 and 500 000 workers participated in the Pretoria/Witwatersrand/Vaal Triangle (PWV) stay-away on 5 and 6 November, and that about 400 000 African pupils stayed away from school.

By the end of the year about 220 00 pupils in various parts of the country were not attending classes.

Individuals involved in left- or right-wing politics were also targets of political violence in 1984. The attacks occurred predominantly in the form of petrol-bombings on homes of individuals. The UDF was accused by leaders of various political parties participating in the Tricameral Elections of perpetrating political violence against people with whom it disagreed. Responing to the accusations, Dr Allan Boesak, patron of the UDF, said, 'It is an act of violence to raid people's houses, to deny young people education, and to pass laws which deny people their humanity. It is not the UDF, but the South African government which perpetrates violence.' The South African Institute of Race Relations (SAIRR) issued a statement condemning the petrol-bomb attacks on African, coloured and Indian communities and some labour leaders in Johannesburg. 'Nothing can justify the attacks,' said the Institute. 'There are few acts more cowardly than the pre-meditated hurling of petrol-bombs into defenceless people's homes in the middle of the night.'

In August, following a petrol bomb attack on the home of Mrs Lucy Mvubelo, a trade unionist, the killing of a Soweto policeman, and petrol-bomb attacks against five candidates in the Tricameral Elections, Brigadier Herman Stadler, a security police officer, claimed that policemen and people seen to be supporting the system were immediate targets of the ANC. A group calling itself the South African Suicide Squad (SASS) claimed responsibility for the petrol-bombings, which included:

- Five petrol bombs thrown into the home of an eighty-two-year-old Soweto councillor, Walter Nqoyi on 5 March.
- On 31 May an eight-year old child, Jabulani Mthembu, was severly burnt and his sister Phindile's hair set alight when one of the three petrol-bombs landed in the bedroom they were sharing with other children in the house of their grandfather, Nehemiah Mthonjeni, a former Soweto councillor.
- A dry-clean depot belonging to the mayor of Soweto, Ephraim Tshabalala, was severely damaged in a bomb attack on 6 August.
- Patrick Gaboutloeloe's home was attacked for the fourth time on 14 June.
- On 6 September a petrol bomb was thrown into the bedroom of the nineteen-year-old daughter of Don Mmesi, the mayor of Dobsonville.

Councillors were not the only targets of SASS and other petrol bomb attacks. Other individuals seen as 'part of the system' or with whose views the unknown persons disagreed, were also attacked. They included trade unionists, policemen, school principals and religious personalities.

Undaunted by the increasing violence and perhaps encouraged by the increasing public involvement, Cosas faithfuls stridently chanted, 'Forward, forward to a democratic people's education,' and 'Long live, long live the education struggle.' For its part, the government remained convinced that it would stem the tide. So it seemed, at least, to me.

CHAPTER 14

REDEEMING THE BLIGHT OF
BANTU EDUCATION

It is worth recording, I reckon, that despite all the gloom and sordidness overwhelming the country, there were other forces, perhaps generally less well-known politically, which were involved, each in its own particular way, in the educational struggle in the 1980s. These forces were created somewhat out of desperation by concerned educationists who were not only keen to redeem the blight of Bantu Education, but also realised the country would need enlightened manpower in order to fulfill the promise of a better, brighter future.

Those forces, seldom in the limelight and therefore less well-known to the general public, included Project Matriculation (PROMAT), Programme for Technological Careers (PROTEC), Khanya College, and the Council for Black Education and Research. (One of the points that had clearly come out of the 16 June Soweto uprising was that black teachers countrywide were under-qualified and, therefore, their teaching ineffective). As a result, there was a great need for teachers generally to upgrade their qualifications. Thus the rise of the somewhat reticent forces namely, PROMAT, PROTEC and Khanya College, all of them involved in formal education, and the council, whose motto was 'knowledge is power for growth,' and which ran informal enrichment educational programmes. They were non-profit-making organisations, which, without financial support from donor agencies, would have remained no more than mere wishful thinking.

> *Established by a white educationist, Larry Robertson, in 1982 to give blacks 'top class' secondary education, PROMAT initially consisted of five colleges around the country, giving about 30 000 people who were teaching without matriculation certificates the chance to matriculate in one year. By 1988 a fully-fledged PROMAT campus – complete with library, hall and lecture rooms – was opened on a farm at Cullinan outside Pretoria. The campus, which also offered in-service training for teachers without matric, was the first privately-run, independent teachers' training college in the country. It has been estimated that the education of around one million black children was enhanced because of the training PROMAT gave to their teachers.*

[*Collected South African Obituaries 2005*, Chris Barron, Penguin Books]

Also started in 1982 in Soweto to help school-leavers to prepare for and successfully embark on careers in science, engineering and technology was PROTEC. The programmes provided supplementary education for Standards 8, 9 and 10 learners. Its main operations involved implanting a series of educational projects throughout the country, focusing on teacher training; school improvement in science, mathematics, technology, information technology curriculum and English education; and school management training. By 1990 PROMAT was running programmes in twenty-six black communities. The organisation is today a leading provider of teacher training and curriculum support in school-level technology education and provides materials, teacher training and school-level quality assurance for science, maths and computer education.

It has supported the education of over 160 000 students from

Standard 2 to Matric in over 900 schools and has trained and supported more than 4 500 school managers and teachers, according to a marketing document of the organisation.

Then there was Khanya College, started in 1986 by educationist John Samuel, director at the time of the South African Committee for Higher Education (SACHED). It was involved in numerous other educational projects, including a basic adult education programme. The college prepared poorly-qualified, community-conscious matriculants for university studies and facilitated their eventual tenure at university. The college offered students a one-year, full-time study programme. They studied two courses at first-year university level through lectures, group work, discussions, readings and group projects. They were encouraged to develop an independent, critical perspective, and were assisted with any reading, writing and study problems they had. Students could choose any two of the following courses: African Literature, African History, Economics, Mathematics, Physics and Sociology.

The college had two campuses – one in Johannesburg and the other in Cape Town. There were no cooks and cleaners hired to work at the students residences at the two campuses. Students had to do the cooking and cleaning themselves, and in order to perform these duties well, the students organised themselves.

Most of the students who enrolled at the college were members of Cosas, including those who, because of their involvement in political activities, had not been able to write matriculation examinations. Even those who had failed to qualify for university were admitted for study at Khanya College. If they successfully completed their courses at the college, they would be ready to enter university. The college had entered into agreement with the universities of the Witwatersrand, Cape Town, Rhodes and Natal to accept students who completed their courses at the college.

The Council for Black Education and Research was founded in 1981 by a group of teachers – among them Lekgau Mathabathe, a

167

former principal of Morris Isaacson High School in Soweto; Fanyana Mazibuko, also a former teacher at Morris Isaacson; and Professor P. Mohanoe of Turfloop (the University of the North) in Pietersburg (now Polokwane) – under the leadership of Es'kia Mphahlele, the then-professor of African Literature at the University of the Witwatersrand in Johannesburg (Wits).

Professor Mphahlele canvassed countrywide for support for the council. He told a two-day conference, held at the central Methodist Church in Durban in 1981 and attended by educationists from the Eastern Cape, Natal, Orange Free State and Western Cape (including universities of Cape Town, Transkei, Turfloop and Bophuthatswana), that:

> *As a result of the present social climate that affected schooling, Soweto Teachers' Action Committee had thought it fit to create an organisation that would inspire in our society a creative urge based on sound, relevant research into education. Black South Africa was way, way behind other African countries in scholarship. We have now to make our presence felt as a thinking people. We have, at one level, to go beyond the bare political statement about the condition of our education, and, at another level, to snap out of our zombie condition. This we can only do by institutionalising our intellectual activities. If we don't, we are doomed.*

Throughout 1982, for instance, the council ran a series of lectures under the theme *Know Your Continent – Africa,* at the university of the Witwatersrand. The lectures were held on Saturdays from 10am until 12 noon. Although ninety participants were enrolled, attendance fluctuated between twenty and sixty throughout the twenty-eight weeks. Lecturers who contributed to the series were: Professor Phillip Tobias, head of the medical school at Wits; Professor Charles van Onselen, director of the institute of

African studies at Wits; Professor Es'kia Mphahlele himself; Dr Phillip Bonner, lecturer in politics at Wits; Dr Tom Lodge, a lecture in politics at Wits; geographer Mr Phillip Mokoko of the South African Committee for Higher Education; Professor Khabi Mngoma, head of the department of music at the University of Zululand; Dr Tim Couzens of the department of English and comparative literature at Wits; and Mr Lebamang Sebidi, lecturer at the University of South Africa and at the Wilgespruit Fellowship Centre. Mrs Joyce Siwani and Mr Julius Mtsaka produced a one-act play for participants.

The year 1983 opened with a BBC film, the *Ascent of Man,* written and presented by the famous mathematician, Professor Jacob Bronowski. The average attendance at the showing of the thirteen one-hour segments of this most elevating and enlightening film was twenty persons. Another thirteen-part film, *Life on Earth,* which pulled together studies in natural sciences and geography suitable for high schools, was also screened at the Bridgeman Centre in Zola, Soweto.

Not only did we learn from the series of Africa's own contribution to world history, of her own social history and social geography, the existence of African kingdoms and governments long before colonisation, gold mining by indigenous African societies, the discovery of diamonds and gold in southern Africa and the effect of the subsequent large-scale mining on inhabitants within the region after the continent was colonised. But, above all, we also learnt what our cultural heritage was to our own development as a people, a people of African origin and descent. We learnt something, too about our own people who pioneered African writing in South Africa in the early nineteenth century.

The council moved from Wits to the Funda Centre in Diepkloof, Soweto in 1984, whence another long series of lectures, *Know Yourself,* was begun. It was in Soweto, too, that the council began publishing its journals – *Education Press* and the *Capricorn*

Papers. Education Press published general news items in education, while some of the delivered lectures were published in the *Capricorn Papers*.

All these, needless to say, were efforts born out of the realisation that democracy could be meaningful only if the people attained good education and some deep understanding of their history. These organisations laboured tirelessly in the midst of the unfolding chaos, in earnest preparation for the future. Some parents and community leaders, particularly in Soweto, were just as concerned that schooling in the townships was being crippled, if not already paralysed. They made arrangements with sympathetic white school principals in the suburbs for black children to be allowed to attend classes at their schools when the normal schoolday ended each day. Did the political activists chanting, 'Forward, forward to a people's democratic education' in the streets take kindly to these efforts? No. This explains the emergence within their ranks at the time of the terrible slogan, '*Liberation first, education later.*'

CHAPTER 15

THE STRUGGLE TAKES CONCRETE FORM AT LAST

The government was cracking the whip in all directions. Louis le Grange, Minister of Law and Order, renewed the ban on open public meetings for a further year by notice in the government gazette on 30 March 1984. In September the ban was extended to all indoor gatherings for the period 12 to 30 September in twenty-one magisterial districts, mostly in the PWV area. The banning took effect on the seventh anniversary of the death in detention of Steve Biko.
[Race Relations Survey 1984, SAIRR, Johannesburg]

A number of more specific bans were also imposed. In Cradock in the Eastern Cape, for instance, all meetings were prohibited for six months from the end of March. The UDF and all its affiliates were prohibited from holding meetings on the last weekend in July in East London. Meetings of UDF affiliates were also the main targets of bannings by magistrates in Johannesburg, Vereeniging, Vanderbijlpark, Sharpeville, Seshego (Pietersburg), Port Elizabeth, Uitenhage, East London, Queenstown, Mdantsane (Ciskei), and Zwelitsha (Ciskei). At least eighteen funerals were restricted to taking place only on specific dates at specific times, with limits on the number of mourners who could attend. This action was taken by magistrates in Johannesburg, Benoni, Heildelberg, Alberton, Verulam (north of Durban), Port Elizabeth, Grahamstown,

Uitenhage, East London, and Mdantsane.

On 4 August forty people were arrested at a church in Mdantsane for allegedly holding a gathering despite a ban in terms of the Ciskei National Security Act of 1982, which prohibited gatherings of more than five people from 1 August until 6 August (in addition to the general ban in the Ciskei of all gatherings of more than twenty people). On 29 August all political gatherings in Venda were banned for nineteen days, covering the fifth independence celebrations, under the Riotous Assemblies Act of 1956. A three-day church workshop on rural poverty to be held at Thaba Nchu (Bophuthatswana) was banned on 10 October. The Transkei authorities outlawed the UDF, Cosas and Azaso in October, in terms of the Transkei Public Security Act of 1977. The UDF said that none of the prohibited organisations was officially constituted in the Transkei.

There were calls on the South African government to lift the bans on the ANC and the PAC, both of them listed as unlawful organisations in terms of the Internal Security Act. The mayor of Alexandra (Sandton), Rev Sam Buti, in a letter to the Prime Minister PW Botha, was among those making such calls. The pastor also asked the government to invite the ANC and PAC to take part in the talks. Botha turned down the request, saying that it was 'out of the question' as he had 'irrefutable evidence' that these organisations were 'being used by the Communist powers to further their own ends.' [Race Relations Survey 1984, SAIRR, Johannesburg] In September the synod of the Nederduitse Gereformeerde Kerk in Afrika (NGKA) also called for the bans on the two organisations to be lifted. The council of the South African Institute of Race Relations also took a resolution at its annual general meeting in September calling for the lifting of the bans on the ANC, the PAC and the seventeen Black Consciousness organisations banned in October 1977. At the same time the SAIRR called for an amnesty for leaders 'serving prison sentences for essentially political offences' and freedom for political exiles to return home 'subject to their renunciation of violence. '[Race Relations Survey 1984, SAIRR, Johannesburg]

At the end of December 1984, eleven people, including Winnie Mandela and journalist Mathatha Tsedu, were restricted under the provisions of the Internal Security Act. A total of 530 people were, according to the government, detained in terms of security legislation.

In January 1985 various branches of Cosas called on pupils to continue class boycotts in protest against the continued detention of fellow pupils. In March Cosas rejected the constitution for SRCs drawn up by the Department of Education and Training, demanding that students should have been invited to participate when the constitution was being composed. In May Sipho Mutsi, an Odendaalsrus (Orange Free State) pupil and Cosas organiser, died in detention. In July police raided the homes of Cosas members, detaining many.

On 20 July, following continuing unrest and disturbances at midnight in many areas within the country, a State of Emergency was declared in thirty-six magisterial districts. On 28 August Cosas was banned.

Subsequently, Louis Le Grange, Minister of Law and Order, said:

> *After I have considered a factual report and recommendations made to me by an advisory committee in terms of a section of the Internal Security Act of 1982 regarding the organisation known as the Congress of South African Students, I have decided to declare that organisation to be an unlawful organisation in terms of Section 4(1) of the said Act.*

[Race Relations Survey 1985, SAIRR, Johannesburg]

The banning, which affected pupils in specific areas in the

Eastern Cape and in the PWV region, was condemned by, among others, the United States government, UDF, Nusas, and Azasm (Azanian Student Movement). A Progressive Federal Party member of parliament, Ken Andrew, in a newspaper interview, described the banning as 'unjust, stupid, short-sighted, and likely to be counter-productive.' The ban led to an increasing number of organisations of pupils, under the umbrella of Azasm, being formed. The boycotting of classes by pupils demanding the introduction of the formation of SRCs continued regardless. 'Lack of satisfactory resolution of SRCs has led to a deepening of the education crisis,' said Vusi Khanyile, convenor of the National Co-ordinating Committee of Parents' Committees (NCCPCs), which had been negotiating on behalf of pupils with the education department.

The banning orders stipulated that no pupils should, among other things, be outside their classrooms except during break or for the purpose of visiting a dressing room or changing classes; no pupil should, on any school day, while being on school premises, partake in any activities not supervised or ordered by a member of staff, and which did not have direct bearing on his/her tuition at such a school; no person who was not a pupil at, or was not employed at, a school in the specific areas should, at any time, enter or be on the premises or in the buildings of such a school; and a member of the South African Police, the SA Railway Police, the SA Defence Force, or the prisons service could, at any time, with regard to a certain person, school, or matter, grant exemption from any of the restrictions of the banning orders.

It is noteworthy that, despite these Emergency Regulations, which were intended to confine pupils to their classrooms, African pupils continued boycotting classes, demanding the release of detained pupils, and the introduction of democratic SRCs. On 28 August Cosas was banned, sparking off a call by Azaso for pupils to boycott classes, demanding that the ban be lifted. At the beginning of September the divisional commissioner of the SAP in Soweto,

Brigadier Jan Coetzee, said that the Emergency Regulations were not working and blamed Cosas for the situation. The situation in Soweto, he said, had improved 'slightly' but deteriorated from 30 August because of 'Cosas activities', He denied that the presence of security forces near schools created 'excitement' among pupils, making some of them fear going to school. Unless someone had a guilty conscience, he said, there was no reason why the presence of security forces near schools should create problems for anybody.

> *According to the Department of Education and Training 674 275 African pupils at 907 primary schools were affected by school boycotts in 1985. A total of 230 secondary schools out of 323 registered post-primary schools were also affected. About 360 000 coloured pupils were affected by school boycotts too. Altogether 294 African schools were damaged, at a cost of R7, 8 million.*

[Race Relations Survey 1985, SAIRR, Johannesburg]

On 26 October, the State of Emergency was extended to eight other areas. On 3 December 1985, and 7 February 1986, it was lifted in eight and six magisterial districts respectively. The State of Emergency, which lasted 229 days, was lifted on 7 March 1986. Altogether 7 996 people were detained under the Emergency Regulations, of whom 3 681 were under twenty-one years of age. This was the second time in the history of South Africa that a State of Emergency had been declared, the first being in 1960 when 122 magisterial districts were affected.

Attacks on anti-apartheid activists had also become widespread throughout the year. The UDF, whose members seemed the main targets, alleged that 'Gestapo tactics' were being used against opponents of the State. Azapo was also a major target. The Eastern Cape, which was the major unrest area, was also the main area of attacks on anti-apartheid activists.

In January 1985, the visit to South Africa of an American senator, Edward Kennedy had exposed divisions between the UDF and Azapo. While the UDF hosted Senator Kennedy in certain places, Azapo and the Cape Action League – both of them affiliates of the National Forum Committee (NFC) – staged protests in Johannesburg condemning his visit. In Soweto, a meeting hosted by the Anglican Bishop of Johannesburg, the Rt Rev Desmond Tutu, at the Regina Mundi Church was disrupted by members of Azapo and Action Youth, which was also associated with the NFC. In consequence, the Kennedy meeting was called off. In the same month and perhaps in retaliation, UDF supporters disrupted a meeting in Tembisa in the East Rand that was organised by Azapo to form a new branch of its student wing, The Azanian Student Movement (Azasm).

The homes of a number of UDF activists in the Vaal Triangle were petrol-bombed at the end of February. Azapo pamphlets were found at the scene of attacks. Both the UDF and Azapo blamed 'agents of the state'. In mid-March, the home of a Soweto Youth Congress (SOYCO) member was petrol-bombed. The homes of two UDF leaders, the Rev Frank Chikane and Aubrey Mokoena, and those of UDF members in the Eastern Cape were also petrol-bombed. At Thabong in the northern Orange Free State, two members of Azasm had their homes petrol-bombed. Homes of Azapo, Azasm and Cosas were petrol-bombed in Zamdela (Sasolburg, Orange Free State) and in Grahamstown (Eastern Cape). Early in June, the homes of three Azapo members were attacked with petrol bombs, while four officials of the Cradock Residents Association, Messrs Matthew Goniwe, Fort Calata, Sicelo Mhlawuli, and Sparrow Mkonto, were murdered by unknown assassins. (Of course, we now know the murderers were members of the security forces.)

In August a lawyer and UDF officer-bearer, Victoria Mxenge, was killed in Umlazi (Durban). In the same month, three leading members of the Port Elizabeth Black Civic Organisation (Pebco), disappeared. They were Messrs Sipho Hashe, Qagawuli Godolozi and Champion Galela. The body of a UDF activist, Toto Dweba, was found on the Natal north coast. The home of a Communist leader and UDF sympathiser, David Gasa, was burnt down in Umlazi, also in August. In September an organiser of a UDF affiliate, the National Federation of Workers, was killed in Durban, and the home of Natal Indian Congress member, Dr Fatima Meer, was attacked. Four people died in attacks in townships in Durban in October. There was also an attempt on the life of a Durban Communist leader, Aubrey Nyembezi. The Cape Town offices of the UDF and emergent trade unions were burnt. The home of the Watson brothers, whose shops were exempted from the consumer boycott in Port Elizabeth because the white brothers were seen as anti-racist, was petrol-bombed in mid-October. Towards the end of October two UDF activists, Ngwako Ramalepe and Batandwa Ndondo, were allegedly killed by plainclothes policemen in Lebowa (northern Transvaal) and the Eastern Cape respectively.

Ishmael Mkhabela, the Azapo president, said on 14 May that since the beginning of the month four members of his organisation had been killed, nineteen attacked, and thirteen arrested, while thirty-three homes of Azapo members had been burnt, all in connection with the conflict between the UDF and Azapo. He said, 'Under the cloak of a general civil uprising, the UDF has shown its hand in pursuance of its grand hegemonic ambitions of the liberation struggle.' Azapo remained committed, he added, to all constructive measures to resolve the conflict between the two organisations. And in a letter to Azapo, the UDF national executive said their mutual repugnance of apartheid superseded their differences. The conflict continued, however.

During clashes between Inkatha Yenkululeko Yesizwe (Inkatha Freedom Party) and the UDF in Natal in May, the homes of six UDF supporters were destroyed at Hambanathi in Durban. Chief

Mangosuthu Buthelezi, president of Inkatha and chief minister of KwaZulu, claimed that the UDF was trying to create 'no go' areas for him in Natal. The ANC claimed in September that Chief Buthelezi had 'unleashed' the *amabutho* (impis) against students. In October, Chief Buthelezi attacked the ANC and the UDF as being the 'frontline actors' in the 'butchery' of those who opposed them.

As violent conflict within black communities continued, vigilante groups emerged. In some instances such groups imposed relative stability, but in others they exacerbated conflict. Vigilantes were organised in some cases to defend some blacks against violent attacks by others, but in other instances they initiated conflict. Despite diverse reasons for the formation of the vigilante groups, their attacks were primarily directed at anti–government militants. Writing about the wanton township violence in her book, *Open Earth and Black Roses* (2001), Sibongile Mkhabela, nee Mthembu, (student leader who, together with ten male student leaders, was convicted for sedition in May 1977 following their political activities) says:

> *The conspiratorial silence of the church and the ranks of the black leadership was deafening. The 1980s were marked by the absence of a clear, bold, principled and values-based direction within the black community. Grassroots leaders, parents and other lower-tier leaders were intoxicated with their new-found power or were disempowered by shallow and dangerous slogans and new struggle practices that marginalised them.*
>
> *The political and church leadership of the day swayed in confusion as it tried to be politically-correct. When young people with little direction started destroying human life, some leaders were quick to christen them Young Lions. The Young Lions and others who responded to their acts, which bordered on anarchy, were devouring the flock, heaven's sake!*

The need to gain political support for one's group, as though we had already won the space to elect representatives, was too great. If the issue was fundamentally ideological, it could have led to one approach that could build on what was common among the fragments of the liberation struggle. No, the issue was about winners and losers, and the losers had to die. Political turf was to be won at all costs.

I believed then, against growing odds, that black leadership was not supposed to be divided or justify what happened. They were simply supposed to acknowledge what happened so as to draw lessons for future generations. We must acknowledge that when we did not protest at the murder of someone who differed from us ideologically, even a hated government-appointed community councillor, we taught our children not to value human life. When we sat silently as students undermined their teachers and we became quiet when kids accused parents of being sell-outs, we unwittingly endorsed and encouraged disrespect for our own values and encouraged the growth of unguided activism.

In declaring a State of Emergency on 20 July 1985, state President PW Botha had stated:

Every responsible South African has, with growing concern, taken note of conditions of violence and lawlessness which, in recent times, have increased and have become more cruel and some more severe in certain parts of the country especially in black townships. These acts of violence and thuggery are directed at the property and persons of law-abiding black people, and take the form of incitement, intimidation, arson, inhuman forms of assault, and even murder. Thus far, the government has shown the utmost patience. However, I cannot ignore the insistence of all

> *responsible South Africans, especially the black majority, who*
> *ask that conditions be normalised and that they be granted*
> *the full protection of the law to continue their normal way of*
> *life. It is the duty of government to ensure that a normal*
> *community life is re-established and that community services*
> *are efficiently rendered. Children must be able to receive*
> *tuition. The life and property of all people must be protected,*
> *and law and order must be maintained. In view of the*
> *prevailing conditions, it is essential that the situation be*
> *normalised in such a way that the climate for continued*
> *dialogue in the interest of all people in the constitutional,*
> *economic and social fields is ensured. Against this*
> *background, the government has decided to proclaim a State*
> *of Emergency.*

Needless to say, it had no effect, none whatsoever.

The disinvestment campaign, calling for the international community to withdraw their businesses from South Africa, began in 1984, with Bishop Desmond Tutu as the leading spokesperson for the oppressed masses. It was hugely influenced by the declaration of the State of Emergency in July 1985, and already begun biting. A total of 121 British local authorities were reportedly involved in anti-apartheid activities. Such activities included, for instance, banning purchases of South African products; banning advertising of South African products; withdrawing accounts from banks dealing with South Africa; promoting cultural boycotts against South Africa; putting up anti-apartheid displays in public libraries; honouring opponents of apartheid; banning official visits from South Africa; and developing public understanding of the political situation in South Africa.

A total of forty cities, states and universities in the United States had by November 1985 passed measures authorising the sale of an estimated R3, 5 billion in shares in local companies involved in business in South Africa. As a result of pressure in the United States congress, the American president, Ronald Reagan, reluctantly agreed to limited sanctions against South Africa. The prohibited transactions included the making or approval of bank loans to the South African government; the export of computers and related goods and technology to certain government agencies and any apartheid-enforcing entities of the South African government, with certain narrow exceptions; the import of arms, ammunition, or military vehicles produced in South Africa into the United States; and the extension of export marketing support to United States firms employing at least twenty-five persons in South Africa, which did not adhere fair to labour standards.

According to the Investor Responsibility Center at least twenty United States companies ended or had started winding down their South African operations during 1985. New investments had virtually stopped and investments sold by American universities in the same year alone amounted to $173 million, the total since 1978 being $292 million. It added that most analysts agreed that both economic and political factors were responsible.

It was in a climate pregnant with hopes of increasing worldwide support for the liberation struggle and deepening crisis in education, with threats that 1986 would be declared a 'black year' with no schooling at all, that the Soweto Parents Crisis Committee organised a broad-based two-day consultative conference on education at the University of the Witwatersrand in Johannesburg, beginning on 28 December 1985. Over 600 delegates from different parts of the country crammed the university's Great Hall to hear the two scheduled speakers: Rev Smangaliso Mkhatshwa, a Roman Catholic pastor, and Anglican Bishop Desmond Tutu. However, Lulu Johnson, president of the recently banned Cosas, was also allowed to address the conference and so present the young people's view.

In his presentation Mkhatshwa explained that resistance to

Bantu Education was initially led by parents and teachers in the 1950s. But by 1976/77 the struggle was led by the youth; the adult population was excluded. The most important issue though was that no individual leader, organisation or group should act in isolation at that point. Alternative education, he asserted, prepared people for total liberation; economic and political life.

By alternative education, he said, he referred to people's education. Among other things, the Roman Catholic pastor called for education for liberation, saying that education could not be discussed outside the socio-political setup. 'The struggle, therefore, is for a national democratic society which advances towards socialism and socialism cannot be attained unless the people govern. As a people we need to know where we are, what our strengths and weaknesses are, and what kind of growth has taken place,' he said.

The Cosas president, Johnson, told the gathering, among other things:

> *All we want parents and teachers to understand is: ours is a struggle for better education, the people's education. The Freedom Charter explains it clearly: 'The doors of learning and culture shall be opened to all.' We are quite aware the enemy is not sleeping. Day and night they are discrediting our struggles as being waged by radicals not concerned with education. It is not the case. We have always and are still concerned about education. The regime has imposed a system of undemocratic and racist education which is biased in favour of the interest of the ruling class. The very same education system makes us ignorant. It is thus ignorance that we wage war against. Tooth and nail, we will relentlessly fight our war to the bitter end. The chains will be broken by our consistent fight for a people education.*

Johnson said it had become clear that the government could not run the 'show' alone. Thus the intervention of democratic alternatives 'becomes crucial when we reach a stage of dual power.' What they wanted at that moment was: official recognition of democratic SRCs; lifting of the State of Emergency; unconditional release of all detainees; unconditional reinstatement of all teachers and re-admission of all students; an end to victimisation and harassment of teachers and students; and the rebuilding and repairing of schools.

The student leader, who had prefaced his address with an attack on 'our education system', which was a product of colonialism and promoted capitalist interest, said that their demands emerged from their own experiences. 'Now we are confronted,' he stressed, 'with a situation in which our counterparts in the coloured and Indian communities will be expected to show their contribution. At this conference, therefore, we must not allow coloured and Indian education systems to be treated as separate entities of our struggle.' It must be clear to both parents and teachers that the years lost in education and the lives sacrificed were not in vain. They would be avenged.

'We said to the education authorities,' he added, 'open the doors of learning and culture to all; our education system must be free, dynamic and compulsory.' There was no reply. Then we resorted to boycott tactics, trying to win the support of our parents, teachers and all other groups with an interest in education. The answer to that was: detentions; closing down of schools, colleges and universities (as is the case in the entire Western Cape and most parts of the Eastern Cape); teargas and shootings that left the young dead (in Port Elizabeth, Mamelodi [Pretoria], etc); and the cold-blooded killings of the unarmed and innocent students (Ngoako in Mabopane [north of Pretoria] and Andile in East London)'.

The terror acts worsened when one of the determining forces in the education struggle – Cosas – was banned, said Johnson. 'Those who learn, must teach; and those who teach, must learn.

Forward to People's Education for People's Power. Amandla,' Johnson ended his prepared speech.

Ironically, parents who took their children out of the township, where schooling had virtually collapsed, to the suburbs to attend classes in white schools at the end of normal school hours, were bitterly attacked by some youths as 'poisoning' their children with imperialist education, and so alienated those children from their own communities. It seemed that these children, who were quite articulate in expressing their inner feelings regarding the political situation in the country, did not want other youngsters to be like them: articulate, confident, knowledgeable. Nothing could have been more absurd!

However, it was Bishop Tutu, who spoke on the second and last day of the conference, who clearly showed the way. Not only was he forthright, precise and pointed in his address, but he also showed great leadership in mapping out exactly what had to be done. Black people, he said, could not afford an uneducated generation. It was Verwoerd who first attempted to deprive blacks of decent education, and it was his hope that he might thereby produce subservient, docile people. So it would be Pretoria who would be rejoicing if black students had another year without education. In any case, who would the skilled people be when liberation came? There surely had to be preparation for post-liberation South Africa. Only in this way would those in exile, in jail, the leaders and those who had paid a heavy price, not be betrayed.

'The struggle must be flexible and methods must be constantly reviewed. For instance, boycotts were a very useful weapon to highlight the schools crisis. Care must be taken, however, to avoid divisions. In order for a strategy to be enthusiastically and whole-heartedly supported, it must be voluntary. There is no room for intimidation or for petrol- bombing of the people by the people,' Bishop Tutu counselled.

Saluting the youth, for 'diagnosing' the problem – that the education crisis was political – and for being prepared to die for it, Bishop Tutu stressed that a distinction needed to be drawn between objectives or goals and strategies. There were short term goals (like freely-elected SRCs and the abolition of corporal punishment), long term goals (like a free compulsory education for all) and ultimate goals like a free South Africa. 'The parents were beginning to show readiness to pay the price for a new South Africa, for a united, non-racial, just and truly democratic society. 'It is only in such a society that people will be educated to develop their full human potential,' he asserted.

In concluding his talk, Bishop Tutu recommended that the conference resolve that students go back to school, but on firm conditions; and that pregnancies, alcoholism and drug addiction could not be afforded. He said that the government should be given three months to meet the following conditions: the establishment of SRCs; the unbanning of Cosas; the release of detained student leaders; the making of arrangements for catching up work that had been missed; the deferment of examinations; and the setting aside of one day a week for 'people's education'. Tutu further said a body should be established to prepare syllabi for a new South Africa; that schools should be handed over to the churches to run since they were more sympathetic to the cause; and the call to scrap ethnic education should be increased to enlighten the people. Additional demands would be: an end to the State of Emergency; the release of all detainees; the removal of the army from the townships and general amnesty for exiles. 'These reasonable requests should be met within three months. If not, parents, teachers and students should all be engaged in a mass boycott/stayaway action to emphasise that we want our freedom and we want it NOW!'

In consequence, the National Education Crisis Committee (NECC) was immediately formed, not only to draw up an Education Charter, but also to watch whether or not the conditions adopted by conference and listed above were met within the stipulated time of three months.

CHAPTER 16

BETRAYAL GENERATED UNWITTINGLY, PERHAPS

Something was hovering in the air in the second half of the 1980s. Some of it was subtle; yet some of it was overt, quite direct. Disinformation – in various forms – surfaced with monotonous regularity. So did posters, booklets and pamphlets with strange messages. The black unemployed, who wandered in towns and cities, hoping to get 'piece jobs' of any kind, even became targets of unscrupulous individuals. All of these stratagems calculated to discredit our reputable black leadership, both at home and in exile, and so stem the liberation tide.

For instance, Bishop Tutu, returning from one of his many trips abroad, was met by an organised black band of anti-Tutu placard-carrying demonstrators at the airport! No sooner had the 1984 Nobel Peace Prize winner edged his way past the miserable demonstrators, than the bubble burst. Curious reporters, who wanted to know who these people were, where they came from and why they were demonstrating against the bishop, discovered that these were the unemployed. They had been 'hired' by a white man from a street in Pretoria earlier that day, given the placards they carried and transported in a truck to the airport! They expected to be paid when they returned to the capital city. Then there were the numerous posters, pamphlets and booklets dropped, usually under cover of darkness, in the streets, at taxi ranks, railway stations and at bus stops in black townships. One anonymous pamphlet, *How Can We Forget*, with a picture of Bishop Tutu as illustration, and said:

> *When our children challenged the police in fierce skirmishes during the 1976 riots, Tutu's children were safely tucked away in comfort at expensive institutions of higher learning overseas, away from the violence; that our children died and some are in exile – destitute, insecure and face an uncertain future, while Tutu's children are well-educated, secure and full of confidence; that Tutu encouraged our children to reject education – that lifetime opportunity of learning – while he is already educated; that today he is calling for sanctions and disinvestment against South Africa. This means that we will lose our jobs, our children will starve, and once again miss that lifetime opportunity of learning. We shall degrade our lives further backwards.*
>
> *Are we so blind not to realise that Tutu is secure in his job?*
> *Are we so blind not to see that he never stays away from work?*
> *Are we so blind not to see that his children are secure and educated?*
> *Are we so blind not to see that he is fooling us once more?*
> *Let us remind ourselves of his hidden betrayals.*
> *And not allow further occurrences!*
> *Stop! Think! And look back – Before we lose everything!!!*

There was also the booklet *Umluleki/Moeletsi* (Adviser), which, among other things, proclaimed in bold letters:

> *Who Are Our Friends? These so-called friends are living among us but*
> *They use violence*
> *They use (the) 'necklace'*
> *They kill us*

They destroy our businesses (sic)
They destroy our homes
They burn our taxis
They destroy our freedom
They slow down reform
They do not really care about a future for us
They have lied to us and used us
*It is time we stop listening to them. Let us join hands to fight
the common enemy.*

Indeed, some were not so subtle, and yet some overt – that was
the second half of the bloody 1980s. But nobody was fooled, really.
If anybody was, it must have been the authors of these masterpieces
themselves.

If Cosas and the UDF were the foot-soldiers of the liberation
struggle in the 1980s, the NECC – in the persons, among others, of
Bishop Tutu, Rev Mkhatshwa, Rev Frank Chikane, Dr Peter Tsele,
also a minister of religion, Dr Beyers Naude, Vusi Khanyile and Eric
Molobi – was its think-tank. The NECC was not only given the task
of assessing government's responses within three months of the
many demands listed at the end of the first national consultative
conference on the education crisis that was held in December at
Wits, but also to draw up an Education Charter for the future. When
Molly Blackburn, a Black Sash campaigner and Progressive Federal
Party (PFP) member of the provincial council of Walmer, was buried
in January 1986, the UDF conveyed 20 000 mourners in buses to
her funeral in Port Elizabeth in the Eastern Cape. The mourners,
demonstrating their acceptance of a 'white democrat', stood for
hours singing and chanting freedom songs during the funeral
service. Tom Waspe, a spokesperson for a national workshop of UDF
affiliates and area committees in the white community, said that
more and more whites were turning to the UDF for solutions to
South Africa's present crisis. In February, the UDF and the Congress

of the South African Trade Unions (COSATU) held a joint meeting to discuss the worsening political and economic situation. After the meeting, the two organisations issued a joint statement saying they had, among other things, discussed the release of Nelson Mandela, the boycott of the Johannesburg centenary celebrations, and an expression of solidarity with township residents affected by the unrest. Not only would they boycott the centenary celebrations, but they would also actively oppose them.

Numerous campaigns, mainly in the Eastern Cape and the Transvaal, in which residents were called upon not to pay rentals and to boycott white businesses, were mounted by the UDF in March. The areas involved in the consumer boycott included Soweto, Alexndra, Duduza, Burgesfort, Duiwelskloof, Phalaborwa, Pietersburg (all in the then Transvaal) and Port Elizabeth in the Eastern Cape. Street committees were also established in Alexandra, Tembisa and Soweto. When the government's Bureau For Information announced it was producing a 'peace song', the UDF appealed to musicians participating in it to withdraw. 'This move, the production of a peace song, is clearly part of the government's campaign to win the hearts and minds of people. No artist worth his mettle can allow his or her career to be blemished by such a shallow political gimmick. We strongly urge our artists not to fall for this ruse,' said a UDF spokesperson.

Hundreds of UDF posters advertising a 'Free Mandela' meeting at the Claremont Civic Centre in Cape Town were pulled down and, said a UDF organiser, 'Not a vestige of the posters remain. This looks like a carefully planned operation by a group with many resources.' A former member of the South African Defence Force (SADF), Moegsien Abrahams, was murdered by a crowd after he was thrown out of a UDF rally in Mitchells Plain in Cape Town. Realising that the government had failed to address their demands adequately, the NECC planned the second national conference on the crisis in education for the end of March.

The consultative conference was initially intended to take place at the University of Natal over two days, beginning on 29 March. However, at the eleventh hour the university refused to allow the conference to be held there. After much run-around in trying to find a venue at both the University of Natal and the University of Durban-Westville, organisers decided to hold the conference in Chatsworth. At about 2am on 29 March, a car belonging to the NECC was gutted and two others belonging to delegates from the Border region had windows smashed. Delegates leaving the Moon Hotel for the Pioneer Hall, where the more than 1 500 delegates and observers who turned up for the conference were still registering, were attacked by armed men travelling in a Kombi at about 10am. One delegate was seriously injured. Two Putco buses, loaded with men armed with assegais, spears, sticks and axes, pulled up outside the Pioneer Hall. Appeals to the security police to protect delegates were in vain. Two people from the impis were killed – one was burnt to death and the other shot – in a clash between the delegates and the armed impis. Altogether twenty-five people were reported to have been injured in the clashes. From Pioneer Hall delegates went to the Allen Taylor Residence where they held the conference overnight.

In his opening address, Dr Beyers Naude, general secretary of South African Council of Churches, appealed to white students, especially Afrikaans-speaking students, to 'break those fetters' leading them to national suicide and stressed the need for united action in the educational, social, religious and labour spheres. 'People's education and freedom go together. It is not only black education that is in a crisis. White education is also in a crisis. White children are being indoctrinated into supporting the interest of the majority [among them],' Naude said, adding that whites had a role to play in the liberation struggle.

Delivering the keynote address, Zwelakhe Sisulu, editor of *New Nation*, told delegates that when the State of Emergency was declared, a situation of ungovernability existed in some areas within the country only, but by the beginning of 1986 the situation was very different. Ungovernability had extended to many more areas. The struggle had survived the period of emergency and beyond. Actions taken against the leadership did not result in the collapse of organisations. Thus they saw the emergence of areas of people's power in a number of townships. Another feature was the highly political character of the struggle and the tendency for the struggle to develop in a national direction. The masses linked local issues with the questions of political power. A set of national demands emerged that transcended regional differences. 'We are at the crossroads in our struggle for national liberation. We hold the future in our hands. The decisions we take at this conference will be truly historic, because they will determine whether we go forward to progress and peace, or whether the racists push us backwards and reverse the gains we have so far made,' Sisulu asserted.

Perhaps on account of the intermittent disruptive battles with *amabutho* (armed impis suspected of being Inkatha members) working in cahoots with the security police, which reduced their two-day conference into a one-day affair, the NECC never got down to drafting the Education Charter. However, the thirteen resolutions adopted included acceptance of the 'People's education' as recommended earlier by the Adhoc Committee. Most of the other twelve resolutions were essentially a re-statement of the demands made at the first national consultative conference in Johannesburg in December 1985. But even as delegates dispersed, it was abundantly clear that education – call it what you will, alternative or people's education – would remain the thread running through whatever campaigns would follow in the coming weeks, months and years.

Dr Frederick Van Zyl Slabbert, a former PFP leader, told a UDF gathering in Johannesburg in April that, historically, apartheid came before violence and that the violence of apartheid had created the violence that opposed apartheid. He called on whites, apparently those who were already members of the UDF, to persuade other whites to come to terms with the ideal of a non-racial democratic South Africa. 'The only way to break the cycle of violence is to destroy apartheid,' Dr Van Zyl Slabbert said. [Race Relations Survey 1986, Part 1, SAIRR, Johannesburg]

Vusi Khanyile, chairperson of NECC, said at an 'education crisis' gathering at the University of Natal in May that the commission had been established to rewrite the English and history curricula. When completed, the rewritten curricula would be handed over to all the education departments. It was hoped all the curricula for all standards at schools would be rewritten in line with the theme 'people's education for people's power' by 1987. The commission, comprising fifteen people, would co-ordinate the activities of various regional committees. Everyone would be given the opportunity of participating in the formulation of the new curricula. He explained further that trade unionists, academics, teachers and parents were represented on the regional committees. Khanyile also hoped the new curricula would be instituted in white schools as well, because white schools also needed an education that would prepare them for a 'people's future'. [Race Relation Survey 1986, Part 2, SAIRR, Johannesburg]

In November, Khanyile announced that the alternative history and English syllabi were almost complete. The implementation of people's education posed a great challenge, he said. He said further that parent/teacher/student associations were being established and consolidated at all schools. NECC structures would challenge the Department of Education and Training for control of schools, he added. 'The struggle to implement people's education involves people's organisations taking control of the administration of education in the interests of the people,' Khanyile asserted.

A lecturer at the Johannesburg College of Education, Michael Gardiner, said that democracy was the prime concept behind people's education; all decisions were made in consultation with all the people affected. He explained that this was very different 'to the hierarchical approach of present education policy, which presupposes a vertical system with instructions from the top. The people's education approach to decision–making made it impossible to think of education as a separate entity, divorced from society and the community.' With regard to classroom procedure, Gardiner said that the people's education approach differed markedly from the conventional approach. 'No longer will a teacher be able to dictate notes, attempt to teach over large classes, or hand out information as though he is the sole authority on a subject,' Gardiner said. Teachers would have to discover how to use the knowledge and potential of pupils themselves, as well as the special skills that might be available among parents or the community at large. Teachers would also need to implement group work and group discussions to draw out knowledge and generate new material.

Aubrey Matshiqi, a member of the National Education Union of South Africa (NEUSA), told a meeting organised by his organisation that the Department of Education and Training had lost control over many schools in Soweto and the Eastern Cape where aspects of people's education had already been introduced. He said that in these schools, time was set aside every Wednesday and Friday for the teaching of alternative education. In some cases, he added, pupils presented papers illustrating the type of history left out of prescribed textbooks. Matshiqi said further that in some schools pupils had 'dismissed' their principals and had appointed staff members of their choice to run the schools. The liaison officer for the Department of Education and Training, Peter Mundell, confirmed that in Port Alfred and East London (both in the Eastern Cape) teachers were implementing an alternative education, and that the teachers were no longer on the payroll of the department. He also said that he knew of campaigns to get rid of three principals in Soweto, but that the affected principals had been re-instated. [Race Relations Survey 1986, Part 2, SAIRR, Johannesburg]

'When black people talk about people's education, it is in the context of their long history of disenfranchisement. They want an end to the unlimited control the government exercised over their educational matters. And in so doing they only want to reclaim what is their inalienable right, namely, the right to have control over their education,' said Rev Lebamang Sebidi, director of the Trust for Educational Advancement of South Africa in an article he wrote in 1986, which was only published six years later. [*Focus on Education,* Winter 1992, Vol. 1 No. 1]

Oupa Ngwenya, political commentator and analyst, queried the call by exponents of people's education for the establishment of parent/teachers/student organisations, arguing that each of the individual stakeholders had its particular and specific role to play in education and that mixing up those roles was likely to exacerbate the crisis. The role of parents, he said, was to uphold, entrench and protect the right of children to education. Anything that threatened this right justified their intervention. In cases of misconduct, parents should ensure children were justifiably dealt with. They should also ensure that conditions conducive to learning did exist at school.

With regards to the role of teachers, Ngwenya felt that for meaningful education to occur, a considerable amount authority should exist and, in schools teachers typified that authority. The authority of teachers that should be acknowledged by both parents and students involved management, control, admission, movement of pupils from one standard to another, evaluation and administration of discipline.

As for students, their role in the education process was to learn, and to act in a representative capacity in cases of disputes with the authority (teachers). Failure to recognise these differences in roles of parents, teachers and students would neither normalise schooling, nor resolve the crisis,' he said. [*Focus on Education*, Winter 1992, Vol. 1 No. 1]

The debate on alternative education raged on and on and on – even after the NECC was banned, in February 1988. It was however overtaken by events, before its resolution, following the release from prison, after twenty-seven years, of Nelson Mandela on 11 February 1990. This move led to negotiations for a political settlement; the ultimate granting to black people of the right to vote; and, finally, the holding (on 27 April 1994) of the first ever non-racial democratic elections that ended up with a black-led government. Exercising for the first time the right to vote, blacks had overwhelmingly swept the ANC – the oldest African party, which had fought the election on a Freedom Charter-based Reconstruction and Development programme, promising a better life for all – into office. No sooner had the ANC gained political power than it enacted the South African Schools Act of 1996.

The main features of that law were: the creation of a single national system with two categories of schools, namely public and private schools; the declaration of compulsory schooling for young people between six and fifteen years; ensuring access for learners to all public schools; the establishment of representative school governing bodies and learner representative councils; the stipulation that school governing bodies should supplement state money to improve quality; and the statement that the schools law was based on co-operative governance and partnership between government, communities and the private sector. In addition, the schools law laid down, among other provisions, that the governance of every public school was vested in its governing body; admissions policy of a school were to be determined by its governing body within 'national and provincial' frameworks; and that the governing body might also determine the language policy of the school. It is also noteworthy that this schools law banned corporal punishment because corporal punishment was considered an 'infringement' of the right of learners and was said to be 'incompatible' with the spirit of partnership and co-operation embodied in the Act. Then there was the announcement by government of an entirely new syllabus, called Curriculum 2005 or Outcomes-Based Education, in March 1997.

Outcomes-Based Education (OBE) aimed at transforming the education system completely. Under OBE learners were, among other things, to be active participants in the learning process; assessed on an on-going basis; involved in critical thinking, reasoning and action; learning integration of knowledge, relevant and real life situations; as well as taking responsibility for their learning, with pupils being motivated by constant feedback and affirmation of their worth.

It is one thing to come up with a single national education system, a grand-sounding syllabus and a campaign, theoretically, intended to promote a culture of teaching and learning, but quite another actually to implement such a system, syllabus and campaign. In my view, the trouble with government is that it wants quick fixes and overnight solutions to complex national problems. In consequence, it appears to be experimenting, and so fails to work out concrete plans for the ultimate resolutions of the huge, complex problems facing the country. (It also seems unaware of the large proportion of blacks, especially in rural communities, who are still illiterate and unable to administer schools; people who still look up to their elected public representatives not only for guidance and direction, but also expect them to act in their interests, particularly in matters of this nature, if not at all times.)

True, a restructuring of the education system is important and long overdue. But how, for instance, do you hope to implement a new system of education without trained personnel; without any prior development of the much-needed manpower? How do you promote a culture of teaching and learning when you have, through your own schools legislation, undermined the authority of both the principal at school, and of parents in the home; when order and discipline are non-existent at school? When pupils are seemingly encouraged to become a law unto themselves?

Of course, there is also the thorny issue of mother-tongue instruction at school. Officially, the right to choose the language of teaching is vested in the individual, and a learner in a public school has the right to instruction in the 'language of his or her choice where this is reasonable.' Remember also that the governing body of a public school may determine the language policy of a school. All this must mean that a parent or guardian can say to the school principal that he/she wants his/her child to be taught, for instance, in Sepedi while a pupil also has the right to choose, regardless of the wishes of his/her parents, the language in which he/she wants to be taught! What happens, for example, if parents and the school governing body want English to be the medium of instruction and children say, 'No, we want to be taught in Setswana or Sepedi or isiZulu?' What will happen in such an instance?

The government has often stated that it is 'disturbed' by indications that the majority of African parents want their children to be taught in English, saying it has neither 'competent' teachers, nor the necessary learning materials; that it fears the choice by parents of English-medium instruction will have a negative impact on both 'performance' of learners, due to lack of 'support inside and outside' for children to cope with the language, and on the children's cultural growth and development.

Black people have, over centuries, been made to believe that education means a mastery of English. This belief has been strengthened since the new political dispensation. Daily, blacks see English being used in the conduct of public affairs. Extensive, if not exclusive, use of English is visible even in parliament, on television and in the radio, and especially in print media. Besides, English is the current language of commerce and industry. Our highly-respected and internationally renowned former president,

Nelson Mandela, uses English at every turn, and so does his successor, Thabo Mbeki. These men are models for parents. Every self-respecting parent would like his/her child to be as proficient in the use of English as the two leaders.

Yes, Africans should, as a people, grow culturally and develop a sense of pride in being who they are. But growth and development cannot be realised overnight. Indeed, there are no short-cuts either in transforming the education system or in developing cultural growth. Careful planning and a deliberate, long-term programme are crucial if we are to achieve our goals – fostering cultural growth and the use of the indigenous African languages in education as well as in the conduct of public affairs.

True, the development of indigenous languages, which were deliberately suppressed over centuries of colonial and apartheid rule, is essential. But to develop them effectively, we need to embark on a long-term programme that entails, among other things, eventual transformation of the language of commerce and industry. For as long as English remains the language of the corporate world, so will African parents prefer English to mother tongue as medium of instruction in schools. The reason for this is obvious: they, too, want their children to be economically functional in their adulthood and, maybe, even become national leaders.

The ruling class cannot realise their dream, no matter how noble it might be, unless they practise what they preach. Why do they want ordinary folk, the common people in the street, to have their children taught through the medium of mother tongue when their own children are attending private schools, where no African languages are offered, even as subjects, let alone being used? When their own children, who are gainfully employed in commerce and industry, boast that they are 'incredibly English'.

Formal education, essential for any people to make progress in the modern technological world, has become too unequal, too expensive and so inaccessible to many an African families today. Most public schools, particularly those in rural communities (where in certain instances children still attend classes under trees), have no libraries, laboratories or electricity, nor water and flush toilets. As an educated black elite, we have betrayed, unwittingly perhaps, all those who placed their trust in us – or so it seems.

Bibliography

1. *Turfloop Testimony: The dilemma of black university in SA;* edited by GM Nkondo, Ravan Press, Johannesburg, 1976
2. *The Super-Afrikaners* by Ivor Wilkins and Hans Strydom; Jonathan Ball Publishers, 1978
3. The national press, especially *The Star, The Rand Daily Mail, Sunday Times*
4. Cillié commission Report, Vol. 1
5. *Mabangalala; The Rise of Right-Wing Vigilantes in South Africa* by Nicholas Haysom; Centre for Legal Studies, University of the Witwatersrand, 1986
6. *Race Relations Surveys* 1979-1990, South African Institute of Race Relations (SAIRR), Johannesburg
7. *School Boycotts 1984: The crisis in African Education* by Monica Bot. Indicator Project South Africa 1985
8. *You and the Rikhoto, Case: A Black Sash Publication*, Topical Briefings and statistical releases: SAIRR, 1982
9. *Cosas National Newsletter,* March/April 1983
10. *Cosas National Newsletter,* October/Nov 1983
11. *Staffrider,* April/May 1981
12. *Reconstruction: 90 years of Black Historical Literature* compiled and edited by Mothobi Mutloatse, Ravan Press, 1981
13. *Umhlaba Wethu;* edited by Mothobi Mutloatse, Skotaville, 1989
14. *From Protest to Challenge: A Documentary History of African Politics in South Africa* 1882-1990. Vol. 5: Nadir and Resurgence, 1964–1979 by Thomas G Karis and Gail M Gerhart, 1997
15. *Open Earth and Black Roses; Remembering 16 June 1976* by Sibongile Mkhabela, Skotaville Press, 2001
16. Unpublished National Education Crisis Committee reports
17. *Focus on Education,* Winter 1992, Vol. 1 No. 1, 1992

18. Unpublished Reports of the Council for Black Education and Research, 1983
19. Khanya College Prospectus, 1994
20. A 2005 flyer of the Programme for Technological Careers (PROTEC)
21. Collected South African Obituaries, by Chris Barron, Penguin Books, 2005

Acronyms

ANC	African National Congress
Asseca	Association for Education & Cultural Advancement of the Africans
Azapo	Azanian People's Organisation
Azasm	Azanian Student Movement
Azaso	Azanian Student Organisation
BPA	Black Parents Association
BCP	Black Community Programmes
BPC	Black People's Convention
Cosas	Congress of South African Students
Nusas	National Union of South African Students
PAC	Pan Africanist Congress
SABC-TV	South African Broadcasting Corporation–Television
SACC	South African Council of Churches
Sasm	South African Students Movement
Saso	South African Students Organisation
SCA	Soweto Civic Association
SRC	Students Representative Council
SSRC	Soweto Students Representative Council
UBC	Urban Bantu Council / Useless Boys Club
UDF	United Democratic Front

Other titles by Jacana:

See a complete list of Jacana titles at www.jacana.co.za